The Motivation Myth

Overcoming the limitations of praise,
compliments, and appreciation . . .

The Motivation Myth

The Simple Yet Powerful Key to Unlock
Human Potential and Create Inspired
Performance and Achievement

Mattison Grey
PO Box 10405
Houston, TX 77206
832.283.2476

Jonathan Manske
5609 Cheetah Chase
Littleton, CO 80124
303.552.7285

www.mattisongrey.com
www.jonathanmanske.com

Cover Design by Clark Kenyon
www.camppopepublishing.com

Published in the United States of America

ISBN-10: 1468151592
ISBN-13: 978-1468151596

To all of our clients ~ past, present, and future ~ who are dedicated to unlocking their full potential and creating inspired performance and achievement.

We have learned and grown through working with each and every one of you. Without you this book would not have been possible!

Acknowledgements

If we tried to acknowledge everyone who has contributed in some way to this book, the acknowledgements would be longer than the book.

Everyone we have met in our life has contributed in some way to this book. We could start with our parents, our 4th grade teachers, that one awesome teacher in high school, the sports coach, or…

We certainly want to acknowledge our thousands of clients who over the years have allowed us to acknowledge them. You all have been our laboratory where we continue to learn more and more about people and hone our craft.

And thank you to our courageous students who trusted that this wacky idea called acknowledgment actually works and went out into the world and used the tool.

We believe everyone we have met and interacted with has had a hand in this book. We want to acknowledge you all.

Thanks to all our mentors and teachers ~ whether in person or through those wonderful things called books. We stand on your shoulders.

To those who actually touched this book, thank you so very much!

Evelyn Parker, Kate Krause, Mary Gaul, and John Morgan for the really great content editing, clarification, and suggestions. Your contributions definitely made this book better!

Carol French for copyediting. We know that our grammar skills have room for improvement.

To our partners, Jaime and Anne, and our kids, Nathaniel, Sierra, and Sabine, who inspire us to practice acknowledgement every day. We hope you are as proud of this book as we are. You are the lights of our lives!

Mattison and Jonathan

Contents

"People will forget what you said, people will forget what you did, but people will never forget how you made them feel." ~ Maya Angelou

CHAPTER ONE

Introduction

Do you have people in your life who under-perform, do not live up to their potential, or fail to use their gifts and talents? Do you ever wonder why?

Do you sometimes under-perform, not meet your own expectations for yourself, or feel like you could be using your gifts and talents more effectively?

Does that frustrate you? If you are like most people, the answer is *yes.*

Here is some good news. In this book, you will find a simple and elegant solution to the problems of under-performance. You will also learn why motivation, as currently practiced, seldom works.

The bad news is that you may have to let go of some very strongly held beliefs and some of your favorite go-to motivation techniques. However, if you are willing to do this, I promise you that the communication tool and the ideas presented in this book will make a very powerful difference for you and for the people around you.

A word of warning ~ *The Motivation Myth* may ruffle your feathers or even have you up in arms defending a sacred cow. You will likely be surprised and might even be upset by some of the ideas and suggestions in this book.

That is okay. Change is challenging and improvement is a lot of hard work. However, I am sure you have had experiences in your life where you have taken on a challenge and in the end it was well worth the effort.

If you are interested in positive change and growth or in learning a new, more effective communication tool, then this book is your opportunity to do just that.

Ok, you are still here. Great!

This book will show you how to improve your communication and influence so that you can really contribute to others in a graceful and positive way. But to do that, we first must expose a myth, a myth that is probably near and dear to your heart.

The myth is that praise, appreciation, and compliments help to improve people and their performance. These motivation and communication tools are routinely used in almost all attempts to help people do better.

But, they do not improve people or their performance! Praise, appreciation, and compliments do not actually do what we think they do. Instead, they produce a far different result, a result that is actually undesirable.

Be prepared. If you are like most people I have worked with over the years, you are probably very attached to your use of praise, appreciation, and compliments. Almost every time I talk and train on this topic some people get defensive. Yet once you understand why, and start to use the alternative, you will love the difference that you see and experience in your interactions with others.

This book shines a light on an established habit that people just take for granted as the right way to do things. People do not even think to question it. Instead, they strongly believe that the use of compliments, appreciation, and praise are best practices to motivate, give attention, create connection, build confidence, parent, manage, lead, and instill belief in another person.

Virtually no one questions whether these accepted practices actually work the way we think they do. I am here to tell you they do not!

In this book, you will discover how to use an amazing and extremely effective tool that allows and supports you to:

- ❖ Inspire others to believe in themselves
- ❖ Convey your belief in others
- ❖ Create positive forward motion and momentum
- ❖ Uplift others
- ❖ Turn underperformance into peak performance
- ❖ Create self-confidence and belief in one's capability and competence
- ❖ Create rapport and like-ability
- ❖ Validate others so that they truly feel seen, heard, and understood
- ❖ Make easy course corrections and make better decisions
- ❖ Make people feel truly acknowledged
- ❖ Create opportunities for self-discovery
- ❖ Deliver objective non-confrontational feedback

That tool is acknowledgement!

I can hear the thoughts in your head: "I know what that is. I already do that. I acknowledge people all the time."

Whatever you are currently doing, I can almost guarantee that it is not acknowledgement ~ not true, pure acknowledgement. Most people have not thought about the distinctions between appreciation, compliments, praise, and acknowledgement. It is very likely that you are delivering compliments, appreciation, or praise and calling it acknowledgement.

Very few people know how to deliver a pure acknowledgement. I will show you how to do that.

Acknowledgement is a very different kind of communication tool and you will soon see why. Acknowledgement is the language of results.

Genuine acknowledgement stops people in their tracks, yet moves them powerfully forward.

The purpose of this book is to do the same thing for you and to teach you how to do it to others.

Regardless of the roles you play in life: leader, manager, parent, student, partner, teacher, trainer, friend, or coach, the material in this book can help you to help those around you.

You can use acknowledgement in both your personal and your professional life. Acknowledgement is a personal growth tool as well as a leadership tool. It can be used equally effectively by parents in their parenting as it can by executives leading their teams. Anyone who works with or interacts with other people can benefit from using this tool!

I am often asked when and where this tool works. My answer is simple and always the same. The tool of acknowledgement works wherever there are people who are working to accomplish something.

ASKING YOU TO DO SOME WORK

Acknowledgement can be used in any interaction that you have with another person. And the "why" and the "how to" are the same whether you are a mom interacting with her child, a CEO interacting with a junior executive, a VP interacting with the new mail room employee, a coach interacting with an athlete, spouses interacting, or a friend interacting with a friend. People are people and they need the same things.

Here is the work I am asking you to do: I use many different types of examples throughout the book. Some of them might not mirror your situation. When that happens, do not just skip that idea. Instead, do the mental work necessary to make that relevant to your life. Ask yourself how *could* this apply to me and to my life?

For example, in chapter 3, I talk about employees not feeling appreciated. "When there is judgment, the first and probably the only thing that the employee really gets is that this communication is not about him or her."

Even if you are not a boss or an employee, this material is still highly relevant to you! In this case, you might substitute child, spouse, friend, or whatever is appropriate for "employee."

For example, "When there is judgment, the first and probably the only thing that *your child* really gets is that this communication is not about him or her." Now this content is applicable to you.

ONE LAST REQUEST

Please keep in mind that learning and improving can be uncomfortable. It is often a frustrating, messy business. So even if some of the things in this book surprise or upset you, I invite you to stay curious and experiment. Try the ideas. See for yourself from your actual experience. Navigate the ideas in this book from your heart, not your head (I know ~ easier said than done). The easiest way to do that is to suspend your judgment, follow the guidelines, take action, and pay attention to the outcomes and results that you produce.

AUTHORS' CHALLENGE

Our challenge in writing this book is to convey something that is experiential. You will never understand the power and the beauty of acknowledgement until you use it. In a book, all we have is words. Our intent is that these words are so compelling that it inspires you to take action and actually start using this amazing tool of acknowledgement.

We (Mattison Grey and Jonathan Manske) have thirty-five plus combined years of experience in coaching, training, speaking, and public seminars in the areas of high-performance, leadership, sales, getting out of your own way, and taking out your head trash. We help people get what they really want.

We use the tool of acknowledgement in our work. We have seen and experienced firsthand, over and over again, the amazing positive impact of pure acknowledgement.

We have worked with high-performance teams, organizations, individuals, athletes, and families ~ liberally using this tool.

So that is our challenge: to condense our thousands of hours of experience into a short, easy-to-read book that will inspire you to integrate acknowledgement into your communication toolbox.

AUTHORS' NOTE

Even more challenging was figuring out how to combine two writers' voices, points of view, and experiences into one clear and cohesive piece of work. To accomplish this we decided to write the book in first person. So you will see "I" rather than "we" or "my client" rather than "Mattison's client" or "Jonathan's client." Ultimately we feel this approach will provide a better reader experience.

We hope you enjoy reading this book as much as we enjoyed writing it.

CHAPTER TWO

Why I Wrote This Book

I am a lifelong student of people and performance. For years I have watched people under-perform, get and stay stuck, fail to access their true brilliance, and live lives of quiet desperation. This all happens because of a faulty belief about what really motivates and inspires us as human beings.

I wrote this book because I could no longer stand by and watch people suffer at the hands of others who continually attempt to use crude and ineffective communication tools to improve the capacity of the people around them.

Our culture believes a myth: the myth that communication tools like compliments, appreciation, and praise actually create positive results in people. They do not. Fortunately, there is a tool that consistently and reliably creates results in people. That tool is acknowledgement.

Over the years, I have watched the power of acknowledgement. I have seen it produce almost magical results in people. Even after fourteen years of working with acknowledgement, I am continually surprised by just how powerful and effective a communication tool acknowledgement really is. Unfortunately, virtually no-body knows how to use it. I aim to rectify that problem.

People who have learned the tool of acknow-ledgement and use it consistently see the tremendously positive impact it has on people. I want other people ~ lots of other people ~ to be able to do this, too.

My intention is to equip you with the tool of acknowledgement so that together we can change the way we communicate and create a communication habit that really serves people and contributes to the quality of their lives.

Here are a few reasons why it is worth the effort to develop the skill of acknowledgement:

- ❖ Acknowledgement is an effective leadership tool and it reinforces positive behavior and actions.
- ❖ You can build stronger relationships (all kinds) through acknowledgement. When you acknowledge others, they feel good about themselves. Pretty soon, they begin to notice that when they are with you, they feel good about themselves. When that happens, people want to spend more time with you and you become a valuable resource for them.
- ❖ Acknowledgement effectively conveys attention, appreciation, being valued, and your belief in another person. These are things that people crave. They get the message that they matter and that you "get" them.
- ❖ Acknowledgement can serve as a guidepost and navigational aid for people who are interested in improving their performance and getting better results.

❖ Acknowledgement provides a way to quickly and easily learn from mistakes and to move on (especially for athletes).
❖ Acknowledgement is a sure-fire way to inspire and support your kids and help them to develop a proactive, solution-focused mindset.
❖ Acknowledgement is a very effective tool to use in sales. British author Stuart Wilde said that what you want to do is make it so that people are naturally attracted to you. Then when they show up, bill them. Acknowledgement makes people want to be around you.

The way people currently communicate often ends up producing a negative result, even though they intended it to be a positive communication. Oftentimes, the other person ends up feeling unheard, unappreciated, insignificant, unimportant, not valued, or made wrong.

The unintended message is that this communication is not really about the other person. It is all about the speaker. It is about what the speaker thinks and his or her opinions and judgments.

Think about that for a minute; it is a mind bender. The vast majority of all communication is intended to be about the receiver, about how smart, beautiful, witty, or capable they are. But in reality, most communication is really all about the person delivering the communication, and what *he or she* thinks about the other person (chapter 4 goes into this in-depth).

The overall consequence of this kind of communication is that vitality, curiosity, motivation, desire, and connection all decrease.

Think about your experience. How often do you leave a conversation feeling better about yourself or having increased belief in yourself? These experiences are the exception rather than the rule.

Acknowledgement is a tool that can change all of that! There is no more effective communication tool for bringing out the best in others. Acknowledgement allows you to be a wind in someone's sail, pushing them towards a great life.

BEWARE! I have been teaching this tool for over fourteen years and have seen this over and over. Almost everyone thinks that they already know what acknowledgement is and how to use it. Then they learn what acknowledgement really is and discover that they have never given a pure acknowledgement in their lives.

The best way to approach this book is to get curious about what this thing called *acknowledgement* actually is. Let go of knowing and discover a new way to communicate. Explore with a beginner's mind. If you do not, you will likely miss the full power and beauty of acknowledgement.

Also, be prepared to feel awkward or confused when you start to learn how to acknowledge. Pure acknowledgement is very different from what you are familiar with. It will feel strange. However, you will soon get the hang of it and even more importantly, you will see the positive impact it has on others. Then, I hope, you will become a true believer in acknowledgement, just as I am.

CHAPTER THREE

The Myth

This book explores the myth that appreciation, compliments, and praise are an effective way to motivate people. Virtually everyone has been trained to believe that these things are effective and are even best practices. But are they really?

The U.S. Department of Labor states that 46% of employees who voluntarily quit their jobs did so because they did not feel appreciated.

One explanation for this statistic is that there are a lot of clueless managers and bosses out there, people who do not understand the value of taking care of their employees and making them feel valuable, important, and appreciated.

Undoubtedly, this is part of the problem. There are still some clueless Neanderthals and people who are new to management out there. But do you really think that the current state of management and management training is so bad that 46% of employees do not receive praise, appreciation, feedback, or compliments? I don't.

Another explanation for this phenomenon is that praise, appreciation, feedback, and compliments do not truly make someone feel appreciated. In this case, the 46% could be receiving (either consistently or occasionally) praise, appreciation, feedback and compliments and yet still not feel truly appreciated.

Tom Rath and Gallup Organizations tell us that 65% of Americans in the workplace report that they were not recognized at all in the last 12 months. They claim to have received zero positive feedback from their boss.

People actually quit their jobs because they are not appreciated. In its *Retention Practices Survey*, The Society for Human Resources Management in Alexandria, VA reports that 79% of employees who quit their jobs cite a lack of appreciation as the key reason for leaving.

Whether it is 46% or 79% of people quitting their jobs due to a lack of appreciation, that is a big percentage.

At first, these statistics shocked me. Then I thought about it.

I just cannot imagine that 65% of bosses are not at least trying to give some sort of positive feedback. I have a hard time believing that these bosses did not say something positive at least once in twelve months - not one single "good job." Even a crusty old curmudgeon accidentally lets a "good job" escape his or her lips occasionally.

I came to the conclusion that it is not that the bosses are not trying. They are. Rather, it is that the employees cannot process or do not hear the positive feedback when they receive it.

WHY CAN'T THEY HEAR IT?

Why is it that the employees cannot hear the positive feedback? Why are the bosses' and managers' efforts not being experienced as positive feedback?

The reason the employees cannot hear it or experience it as positive feedback is because the communication is delivered in the form of a compliment, praise, appreciation, or recognition. As we will discuss at length later, all of these things have judgment attached, which makes it impossible for the intended receiver to hear, much less take in, the feedback as positive. Instead, they hear and feel the judgment, which causes them to get stuck in the unpleasant experience of being judged. Once that happens, whatever else was in the communication gets lost because the judgment dominates their experience.

When there is judgment, the first and probably the only thing that the employee really gets is that this communication is not about him or her. Rather, the communication is about something or someone else. It might be about the person speaking and his or her judgments and opinions. It might be about what is good or bad for the company or that particular team. But it is definitely not about the employee!

The judgment is usually followed by thoughts like, "I never get any individual recognition. My efforts are not appreciated. Why do they not see how hard I am trying? What the heck do I have to do to get some credit around here? I am not important. . . "

With this train of thought running, it is impossible to feel appreciated ~ even if that is what the person giving the praise or appreciation is trying his or her best to do.

Ironically, appreciation seldom makes people feel appreciated. Appreciation is a statement about the speaker and about what he or she appreciates. It is about how the speaker's life has been impacted rather than about the other person. Consequently, the other person does not usually experience a sense of being known and seen for who they really are and for the value that he or she created.

If this does not make sense to you yet, hang on. I will go into this in much greater depth in the next chapter.

THE SOLUTION

This is where acknowledgement comes in. Acknowledgement makes people truly feel appreciated. Yet virtually no one is using this incredibly effective communication tool.

The more chaotic and uncertain the world gets, the more we look for the magic bullet. When it comes to people, acknowledgement is the magic bullet. And yes, this is a bold claim that I can confidently make because I have seen the positive impact of acknowledgement in people's lives!

Acknowledgement is an amazing and unparalleled tool to make people feel good about themselves. Acknowledgement increases their belief in themselves and builds self-confidence and self-esteem. It inspires better performance and an increase in beneficial behavior.

I work with entrepreneurs, salespeople, leaders, executives, and managers. These are people whose job it is to get results. They realize that their results are often dependent on the work and the results of other people. The one common theme with all of them is that they are completely perplexed by other people. They just cannot seem to understand why people under-perform and why their motivational techniques do not work very well or for very long. They do not know what to do.

The simple answer is that most, if not all, of what you have been told about what really motivates people and brings out the best in them is flat out wrong. When you are operating under the influence of a myth, you are not dealing with reality and your results will reflect that!

The dictionary defines a myth as an unproved or false collective belief that is used to justify a social institution. I believe that we live smack dab in the consequences of the myth that praise, compliments, and appreciation work to motivate, engage, and inspire. That, my friends, is why I chose to call this book *The Motivation Myth*.

CHAPTER FOUR

Compliments, Praise, And Appreciation Do Not Work

The intent of this chapter is to educate, share, illuminate, and overwhelm you with information about why compliments, praise, and appreciation do not work. After reading this chapter, it is my hope that you will want to learn how to acknowledge so that you can actually produce the results you are attempting to produce when you use these other communication tools.

This is a challenge because people just assume that praise, appreciation, and compliments do the job they are supposed to do. Virtually no one has stopped and really looked at what results compliments, appreciation, and praise produce. I have.

We have been trained since early childhood that complimenting, praising, and appreciating are the right way to do things and that they are effective communication tools. We have been trained to believe that complimenting, praising, and appreciating are the best way to lead, to parent, to build relationships, and to motivate and inspire people.

But, what if they are not the best ways to accomplish these things?

Because of the belief that complimenting, praising, and appreciating are the right and good thing to do, I almost always experience push back from people when they start to explore this.

First and foremost, I am not suggesting that you never compliment, praise, or appreciate ever again. You are welcome to do these things. (However, after learning what is in this book, I wonder if you will want to.)

People often get defensive or upset when they think that I am trying to take their habit of complimenting away from them. This is not surprising since many people have a lot invested in complimenting and praising. It is part of their daily life. It is how they show others and themselves that they are good, kind, caring, and considerate people.

I am simply offering you another tool for your communications toolbox ~ *Acknowledgement!* You know the old saying, "If all you have is a hammer then everything looks like a nail." If you have a variety of tools, then you can use the right tool for the job and produce a much better result.

Once you start using acknowledgement and see the impact that it has, I predict that you will compliment far less often. You might even quit altogether. I personally have no use for compliments any more. I am not interested in doing damage when I have something else I can use that is far more effective and beneficial. And yes, as you will soon see, compliments often cause damage.

The problem with compliments, praise, and appreciation is that they do not accomplish what we have been taught they accomplish.

We have been brainwashed to believe that it is good and kind to compliment. We mistakenly believe that compliments make people feel good about themselves.

We have also been taught that compliments a. praise inspire more of the same behavior or even spur people on to greater heights.

I recently conducted a survey asking people why they compliment.

Almost unanimously, people's answers included something along the lines of: "To make people feel good" or "To make people feel good about themselves."

The second most commonly expressed theme was to reinforce positive behavior and encourage more of the same.

These are great positive intentions: help people feel good about themselves and reinforce their positive behavior. However, compliments are just not a very useful tool for achieving these results.

Let us take a closer look at why compliments, appreciation, and praise do not really work.

I cannot recommend highly enough that you read Po Bronson's eye-opening article, *How Not to Talk to Your Kids, The inverse power of praise.* You can find it at http://nymag.com/news/features/27840/. In fact, stop right now and go read this article! Really ~ go read it now! I will wait.

THE INVERSE POWER OF PRAISE

Here are some of the highlights from Po Bronson's article:

Parents typically view constant praising as a way to build self-esteem and confidence and as a way to make sure their kids excel. Constant praising is seen as the "right way" to parent. A Columbia University survey

5 percent of American parents believe it is ell their kids that they are smart. The belief cing your kid's "smartness" will guarantee high levels of performance and is a great way to support your kids.

However, research shows that labeling kids as "smart" does not prevent them from under-performing, nor does it build their confidence. In fact, it does the exact opposite.

Kids who are labeled as "smart" are less willing to try something they might not be good at or to learn something new. They also have much less perseverance, are less likely to put forth effort, and become risk averse.

Think about the tremendous dilemma a "smart" kid faces when presented with something he or she does not know or is not good at. "I am smart – therefore, I should already know that. But I do not (how uncomfortable is that?). I should not have to put forth any effort at this because I am smart. If I have to put forth effort to learn, that will prove that I am not smart. Consequently, I am not even going to try. I will play it safe and just stick to what I already know, which proves that I am smart."

How difficult is it to juggle all of that? It creates a lot of stress for these kids and puts them into a double bind with seemingly no way out.

In *The Happiness Advantage*, Shawn Achor states, "A Harvard Crimson poll found that as many as 4 in 5 Harvard students suffer from depression at least once during the school year, and nearly half of all students suffer from depression so debilitating they can't function."

How can that be ~ half of the students at Harvard are debilitatingly depressed? Well, let's think about it.

These students have almost certainly been praised their whole lives for being so smart. They are used to being in the top 1% in school and on standardized tests and being praised for their smartness for being in the top 1%. Consequently, much of their identity is built around being smart.

Then they go to Harvard and their environment changes drastically. Everyone at Harvard was a former top 1% kind of person. Now, all of a sudden, 99% of these students are no longer in the top 1% and 50% are suddenly below average. With all that pressure, they fall hard!

They cannot deal with the paradox that comes from identifying themselves as smart and then not performing like a smart person would. After all, how can a smart person perform below average? Their identity as a person is compromised or even destroyed. Consequently, their world crumbles.

Psychologist Carol Dweck has conducted many studies on the subject of the impact of praise. She has concluded that when we praise kids for their intelligence, we are telling them it is important to look smart. Consequently, they should do everything they can to look smart and not risk making mistakes, which would jeopardize the perception of them being smart and thus cause embarrassment.

Dweck says, "Emphasizing natural intelligence takes it (success) out of the child's control, and it provides no good recipe for responding to a failure."

Dr. Roy Baumeister conducted a study that showed college students who were about to fail a class performed even worse after receiving esteem-building praise.

They did worse!!! They were not inspired to do better! This is the exact opposite effect of what we believe to be the power of praise.

Praise, especially excessive praise, can also impact motivation. Kids will start to do things just because they want to be praised. Rather than doing these things for enjoyment or the benefit, they do them just to hear praise. These kids become addicted to praise and consequently become risk averse and lose their autonomy. They cannot act independently or do anything that might result in a loss of praise. The constant praise is too crucial to their emotional well-being.

Scholars from Reed College and Stanford found that the liberal use of praise created a bunch of problems. Their studies showed that highly-praised students have shorter task persistence, make eye contact to check in with the teacher more often, and their answers express uncertainty because they have the intonation of a question.

These highly-praised students are experiencing tremendous pressure to "get it right." If they do not get it right, how can they be smart? But they are smart ~ after all, they have been told that hundreds or even thousands of times. However, if they are learning something new, how can they get it right immediately? That is almost impossible. Yikes! Think of the pressure this creates for these poor kids. They have to be perfect but, of course, perfection is impossible.

Image maintenance becomes their primary focus. They have to protect their smartness at all costs. This can create some nasty consequences like reluctance to try new things, competition, lying, meanness, and cheating. Those qualities are not exactly what we are trying to create through the use of praise.

Also, praise-seeking behavior implies that kids must constantly prove their worth. That is hard work indeed! And, any mistake upsets the apple cart and creates perpetual feelings of inadequacy because someone else will always be doing better. This can make under-performance or failure devastating.

Failure becomes devastating because these kids have lost their resiliency. The dictionary defines resiliency as the ability to recover strength, spirits, and good humor quickly, and the ability to bounce back. They have lost their ability to persevere. They can no longer pick themselves up when they fall.

Failure is imminent and if a person is scared of failure, then life itself becomes very scary.

The worst expression of this is learned helplessness. If we have no way to navigate out of failure or no belief in our ability to do so, then we will start to believe in the futility of our actions. Consequently, when we fail, we can experience such hopelessness that we respond by simply giving up.

Shawn Achor said, "Study after study shows that if we are able to conceive of a failure as an opportunity for growth, we are all the more likely to experience that growth. Conversely, if we conceive of a fall as the worst thing in the world, it becomes just that."

The ability to respond to failure by trying again and putting forth more effort rather than just giving up is such a valuable trait. Seldom does success happen without resiliency and perseverance.

PERSISTENCE QUOTES

"Nothing in the world can take the place of persistence. Talent will not; nothing is more common than unsuccessful men with talent. Genius will not; unrewarded genius is almost a proverb. Education will not; the world is full of educated derelicts. Persistence and determination are omnipotent. The slogan 'press on' has solved and always will solve the problems of the human race." – Calvin Coolidge

"Energy and persistence alter all things." – Benjamin Franklin

"My greatest point is my persistence. I never give up in a match. However down I am, I fight until the last ball. My list of matches shows that I have turned a great many so-called irretrievable defeats into victories." – Bjorn Borg

"The majority of men meet with failure because of their lack of persistence in creating new plans to take the place of those which fail." – Napoleon Hill

This is just a sampling of famous, successful people who understand the virtue of persistence.

PRAISE DESTROYS RESILIENCY

Excessive praise destroys resiliency and persistence. First of all, praise junkies will tend to stop as soon as they are not receiving praise. Secondly, they will not or cannot try harder because their identity of smartness cannot weather another failure.

Sir Bernard Williams, the most brilliant and important British moral philosopher of his time, said, "Man never made any material as resilient as the human spirit."

Unfortunately, praise, appreciation, and compliments more often than not crush the human spirit.

Once students become addicted to praise, they will need constant reward and constant praise. This need for constant reinforcement does not serve them well. And it creates problems for them when they do not get the praise they are addicted to.

Again, please read Po Bronson's eye opening article for more information about the inverse power of praise at http://nymag.com/news/features/27840/.

Is praising your kid's smartness sounding like such a good idea now? I hope not!

INVERSE POWER OF PRAISE AND ADULTS

Most of these studies mentioned are about kids ~ and what are adults except taller, older kids? The effects are the same on adults as they are on kids.

Consultant and author David Rock wrote an article, *Praise Leads to Cheating?* which appeared in the November 10, 2011, edition of the *Harvard Business Review*.

In this article, Rock said, "Some seemingly innocent organizational practices, like praising people for success, are likely to not only reduce performance and increase cheating but also make people less adaptive at work."

He references a study conducted by Stanford Psychology Professor Carol Dweck. In this study, the "smart" adults were less willing to take risks and were willing to lie to protect their status.

Rock quotes Dweck, "People who are praised for being smart don't want to risk their newly minted genius status, and that fosters static, rigid organizations."

Again, is praising anyone's smartness sounding like such a good idea now? I sure hope not!

But wait. There are more reasons why compliments do not really work.

ATTENTION

Attention is in short supply. I have asked hundreds of people if they are getting enough attention and so far not one single person has honestly replied that they are. Consequently, everyone suffers from attention deficit disorder.

This makes attention a tremendously valuable commodity.

I believe that attention is the most valuable thing we can ever give another person. Attention is interpersonal gold.

Legendary personal development speaker and author Jim Rohn said, "Give whatever you are doing and whoever you are with the gift of your attention."

Have you ever been outside on a cold winter day when the sun breaks through the clouds and the warm sunlight hits your face? Isn't that the best feeling ever?

Pure attention creates that same kind of effect. People blossom under attention. They feel good. They feel validated, appreciated, and recognized.

Have you seen the movie, "Avatar?" In this movie, the Na'vi greet each other with "I see you!"

In case you have not seen the movie, this is not a distracted, "Oh I vaguely see that you are over there." This greeting is delivered with 100% attention and respect. It is saying, "I really see you. I see who you are as a person. I see your heart and your spirit. I see you as perfect, whole and complete."

Genuine attention is such a powerful gift to give to another person.

After a recent volleyball match, I talked to one of my opponents. I had never spoken to this man before, even though we had been playing in the same leagues for many years.

During the match, I noticed he was moving faster, hitting harder, and jumping higher than he had in the past. I also noticed he was not wearing the knee support that he used to wear.

After the match, I said to him, "You are moving faster than you did last season."

It was amazing to watch his face brighten. He must have enthusiastically talked to me for at least ten minutes. The whole time we talked, his face was glowing.

One little dollop of attention from me changed this man's evening. Every time I have seen him since then, he has given me a huge smile and a warm greeting.

Think for a minute about what my comment implied. First of all, I had noticed his play that evening, which meant that I was paying attention to him. Secondly, I was able to contrast his play with previous play, which meant that I had been paying attention to him over time. That is a strong message to send. "I see you!"

When we give a compliment, praise, or appreciation, we think that we are also giving attention to the other person. But are we really? (Lest it seem like I am contradicting myself, in the above story I did not praise, compliment, or appreciate. I made a statement of fact about him that delivered attention. ~ Don't worry, this will all make sense by the end of this chapter.)

WHO IS IT REALLY ALL ABOUT?

When you compliment, praise, or appreciate, who is that really about? Is it about you or is it about the person being complimented?

It is completely about you, even though you are trying to make it about them.

Overtly, it seems like it is about the other person, but covertly, it is all about you and your judgments and opinions. A compliment is always about the complimentor not the complimentee.

The same is true with appreciation and praise. It is about me rather than the other person. "I really appreciate . . . " is about what I appreciate. "Good job" is an expression of my opinion. It is about me.

Compliments are more about the person giving the compliment rather than the person being complimented. Every compliment contains an unspoken element, which is "I think" or "in my opinion."

The compliment, "Mary, you look great today" is really, "Mary, in my opinion, you look great today." Now, all of a sudden, I am the world's foremost authority on looking great. This is more about me than it is about Mary.

If it is all about me, does the person being complimented really receive attention?

When I say, "Bob, that was an inspiring pre-sentation," I am actually saying, "In my opinion, Bob, that was an inspiring presentation." This comment allows me to learn about myself ~ "Wow, I was inspired by what Bob said." This is about me.

Could there have been others who thought Bob's presentation was boring? Of course there could be.

I recently wrote a book review on Amazon about a book that I love. I have applied the wisdom of this book all over my life and it has produced wonderful positive changes. It positively changed the way I work with my clients. I am a huge fan!

I read another person's review of this book. His sentiments were that the book is not worth reading.

If this other reviewer and I had subsequent conversations with this author, the author could hear, "Your book inspired me and changed my life" and "Your book is worthless" within the space of ten seconds.

Neither opinion is about the author. They are about me and about the other reviewer. Our attention, energy, and focus are on ourselves and our words are about our experience. How does this deliver attention to the author? The answer is that it does not ~ even though we have been taught that it does.

One of the people who took my survey on why we compliment said it well, "I am saying what I am feeling at the time." It is about her!

When we get really honest with ourselves, we see that a big part of the reason we compliment is because it makes us feel good about ourselves. Complimenting is a strategy we use to demonstrate to ourselves and to others that we are good, caring, and kind people.

Another survey respondent said, "The result I wish to produce (from complimenting) is that they feel good about themselves and I feel good about myself by making them feel good."

Again, this is all about them, not about the other person! They get to feel good about themselves.

We compliment because it makes us feel good. It gives us an opportunity to be heartfelt and authentic and to express something meaningful. That is all great, but it is about you.

If I pay attention to myself when I compliment, I get to learn about myself and about my opinions and my judgments. I get to learn about what I think and what I like. It is useful to know that stuff about yourself; just do not pretend that it is about the other person. It is about you.

The bottom line is that compliments are a poor vehicle for delivering attention!

PAUL NEWMAN'S EXPERIENCE

Here is Paul Newman's take on this (from Shawn Levy's book, *Paul Newman: A Life*). "Some lady staggers across the sidewalk and says: 'I wanna see your baby blues.' There's nothing that makes you feel more like a piece of meat. It's like saying to a woman: 'Open your blouse, I want to see your t**s.'

"What he resented most was the implication that his success as an actor was just because of his eyes and had nothing to do with his abilities."

Complimenting Paul Newman's beautiful blue eyes made him feel like a piece of meat. It did not make him feel good about himself. In fact, these compliments caused so much resistance in him that he completely stopped signing autographs. What a shame.

SUPERIOR/INFERIOR

All the things people do in an attempt to validate and motivate are actually not about the other person; they are about us and they are judgmental. So the people receiving the praise, appreciation, or compliment have to attempt to wade through the judgment to get to the good stuff and most of the time they cannot do it. Feeling judged distracts them. Nobody likes to feel judged. But that is exactly what we do with compliments, praise, and appreciation: we judge.

Judgment automatically produces a "superior/inferior" dynamic. The person who is doing the judging positions him or herself in a superior position. "I know the way things are and I get to pass judgment" ~ whether it is a judgment of good or a judgment of bad, it is still a judgment.

The other person then becomes a victim of my judgment and opinion. Now he or she has to worry about maintaining my good opinion or taking corrective measures in order to obtain my good opinion. I have become that person's superior.

This is subtle, but it is absolutely what happens. Watching vitality can prove this. Seldom, if ever, do people look brighter, more enthusiastic, more present, or more confident after receiving a compliment, praise, or appreciation. Instead, their vitality goes down. They usually look confused and uncomfortable, and instead of being present, they withdraw into their head ~ trying to get past the judgment. Sometimes people even look beaten down.

Do not take my word for this; go out and compliment, praise, and appreciate. Then pay attention and watch what happens.

Are you feeling angry, defensive, or confused about now? If so, you are right on track. If you are like most people, you have built a big piece of your identity around complimenting and that is now being threatened. We know we are good people because we compliment - so what are we supposed to do if we cannot compliment?

At this point, it might be useful to ask yourself, "What sort of result do I want to produce?" Do you want to serve others or feed your ego and feel good about yourself?

If you want to do something that really contributes to others, something that truly validates them, instills belief in them, motivates, and inspires them ~ then praise, compliments, and appreciation are not the right tools for the job.

Please stick with it. There is light around the corner. There is an alternative.

But first, there are a few more major problems with praise, compliments, and appreciation.

ACTION-ABILITY

Compliments do not produce "action-ability." They do not reinforce positive behavior or encourage more of the same behavior.

Here is why:

A compliment does not address, validate, or acknowledge the role the person played in the situation. Compliments typically do not have anything that a person can really take ownership of or a specific action he or she can repeat.

Take the typical compliment, "You look nice today." What exactly did you do to look nice today? How do you own that?

There is nothing in that statement about what you did to "look nice today." There is nothing you can take ownership for and experience the satisfaction that comes from doing it well.

Your only option to repeat this experience would be to wear the exact same clothes, jewelry, and makeup every day for the rest of your life in order to make sure that you look nice. Remember to get your hair cut and styled the exact same way every day as well.

What about these compliments: "You are so handsome or beautiful" or "You are so smart"?

When you were still in the womb, did you look around and say, "Gosh, my parents are ugly and dumb. I better do a little genetic engineering on myself so that I do not turn out like them?" Or did these traits just happen to be the ones you were born with?

There is nothing repeatable here. There is no forward path of action. There is no "doing" that you can proudly own. There is no feedback about the role you played in this situation. Consequently, satisfaction cannot be created or experienced.

Genuine satisfaction and a sense of accomplishment (two very strong drivers of human experience) can only be experienced as a result of something you have done. Legendary American labor leader Walter Reuther said,

"There is no greater satisfaction than to have done it well."

Compliments do not recognize you for what you have done, for the role you have played. Nor do they help you to recognize strategies and actions that you can apply in the future. Instead, they usually cause confusion about what to do next.

What is your first response when you hear the compliment "Good job?" Usually it is confusion, and you want to know "Good job for what?" You want to know what action you took or what result you produced that this other person thinks is good.

That is the big problem with compliments. They are not about the result you produced or the action(s) you took. Consequently, they do not produce the good feelings we think they do.

As self-help pioneer Maxwell Maltz said, "We are built to conquer environments, solve problems, achieve goals, and we find no real satisfaction or happiness in life without obstacles to conquer and goals to achieve." Compliments have nothing to do with conquering, solving, or achieving.

DISCOMFORT, DISTRUST, MISUNDERSTANDING, AND SUSPICION

The final issue with compliments, praise, and appreciation is that they often produce discomfort, distrust, insecurity, misunderstanding, and even suspicion.

Compliments, appreciation, and praise do not light people up; they put people in their heads. Instead of creating positive feelings like: optimism, self-confidence, vitality, and well-being, they often create negative thoughts like: confusion, doubt, and uncertainty.

First of all, these communication tools create a one-up situation. You are now the authority. You are the judge of the other person's performance, appearance, actions, etc. Perceptually, this makes you better than him or her and naturally creates anxiety because he or she is being judged.

In *The Ultimate Secrets Of Total Self-Confidence*, Dr. Robert Anthony says, "Praise is a value judgment. If you tell someone that he is a 'great person' for doing something for you, you are also saying that he is 'not such a great person' if he does not fulfill your desire."

If you can give a compliment, praise, or appreciation, then you can also take it away. The other person now becomes dependent on something fickle, like your good will, your mood or… This creates insecurity and a fear of loss because it could get taken away. "Will you still love or appreciate me even if I fail?"

Watch the eyes of someone when they receive a compliment. Usually, you will see a startled look followed by a withdrawing. More often than not, people look uncomfortable.

People are suspicious of praise, compliments, and appreciation. How many times have you been on the receiving end of a compliment and immediately your suspicion is aroused? What do they want from me? What are they up to? Are they trying to flatter me? Is this genuine?

What happens so often when you hear something like, "You look nice today?" You get suspicious or uncertain. "Does this mean that I looked bad yesterday?" "Is it really such a shock that I look good?" "Do I normally not look good?" "Oh just wait, he or she is about to ask me for something." You end up feeling suspicious and stuck in your head rather than feeling good.

If you do enjoy being complimented, because some people really do, it is important to remember that you are the exception to the rule. Do not make the faulty assumption that just because you enjoy compliments, everyone does.

Compliments make most people uncomfortable. Again, don't take my word for it. Go give compliments and really watch the reaction in the people you compliment. Chances are that you will see them flinch, squirm, deflect the compliment, deny, discount, withdraw, look startled, embarrassed or uncomfortable, or something of that nature.

MISUNDERSTANDING AND DISTRUST ON THE VOLLEYBALL COURT

Coincidentally, as I was writing this chapter, I had an experience that brings this point home.

At the end of our volleyball match, one of my teammates came up to me and said, "You really played great today!"

I am sure his intention was to be kind and make me feel good about myself. At least I hope that was his intention.

However, that is not what happened – not even close.

His compliment could not land. I could not take it in because I had a very different interpretation of my play.

Immediately, my mind got very busy. "What did he mean by that? Does he think that I am not really a good player but played well today? Is he patronizing me?" I experienced confusion and uncertainty. What I did not experience was feeling good about myself.

In my head, I was able to easily negate what he said. I had a different opinion about my performance. I thought that I played great defense. I had a bunch of blocks, some nice digs, and a diving save that drew some "ohs" and "ahs" from my teammates. On offense, I scored a few points because I hustled to get to bad sets and was able to get them over the net. All of that fits with playing well.

However, I also made quite a few hitting errors. Typically, I make very few hitting errors (maybe one per match). So, hitting numerous balls into the net or out of bounds was out of character for me and certainly does not fit with my definition of playing great.

This brings me back to confusion and uncertainty. "What did he really mean? Am I the weak link on the team and he thinks I need encouragement?"

My experience would have been very different if he had used acknowledgement instead (a preview of the next chapter). "You blocked ten hits. You dove for that tipped ball and saved it. You ran to the set that was 10 feet off the net, jumped and spun 180 degrees in the air, and hit the ball into the far corner for a point." To each of those things I would have thought, "Yes, I did!" And, I would have felt good about myself, which is what my teammate was attempting to create (I hope).

I would have left with a swagger in my step instead of confusion in my head.

JOE'S STORY

Here is another example of compliments being misunderstood. In this story about Joe and his nephew, Simon, the compliments actually backfire. The difference between what Joe was trying to accomplish and what he succeeded in accomplishing is fascinating. What he said and what his nephew heard were two very different things.

Joe, an entrepreneur and adjunct college business professor, hired his young, inexperienced and not-real-talented nephew, Simon, to design his website.

After fumbling around trying college and a few others things, Simon was trying to break into the web design business. Simon heard that Joe had incorporated and was running his own business. Simon asked for a shot at helping Joe design his website. In return, Simon would be cheap labor and they would both win. Joe would get his website and Simon would get experience. Simon said that he could design a complete website to Joe's specifications for $825.

Joe thought Simon could get the job done with a little encouragement. Joe also thought his business could be Simon's "springboard" to bigger things.

Along the way, Joe gave Simon a lot of encouragement and motivation, both verbal and financial.

Joe told him things like: "This looks great - keep up the good work. Thanks for your hard work. I appreciate your efforts on this project. This is coming along nicely."

However, all of these complimentary and encouraging statements were preceded with comments or suggestions about what still needed to be done, next steps, or inquiries about what they had last talked about that was still not taken care of.

Joe's intention was to be complimentary and encouraging, as he could see that Simon was struggling to keep up.

Joe really did think Simon would eventually come through with the results he had promised.

Finally, Joe moved his site to a new developer because it was not close to being finished. Simon was not meeting Joe's needs, nor was he responding to Joe's questions and inquiries on a timely basis.

After Joe told him that he was moving to a new developer, Simon threw all the emails Joe sent about "keep up the great work" (there were many of them) back in Joe's face.

Simon was upset that Joe fired him. Simon told Joe things like: "You said I was doing fine. I thought you liked what I had done! You have already told me that the website meets all your needs."

Based on Joe's misinterpreted attempts at support and encouragement, Simon actually thought he was highly talented and was doing a great job. Therefore, he felt that Joe had treated him wrongly when Joe fired him rather than realizing he was fired for poor performance.

Meanwhile, Simon still writes, asking if Joe wants to re-hire him, and stating that he could really use more money. Joe has yet to respond to Simon's requests for a "loan."

Any time you compliment, praise, or appreciate, you run the risk of that communication backfiring.

So often, compliments, praise, and appreciation end up sounding fake or forced, sounding like manipulation, or sounding like you are trying to sell something. They are easy to negate or discount. You can almost always think of a counter example, and so often that is exactly what people do.

In his article, Po Bronson discusses how children "scrutinize praise for hidden agendas." Children over the age of seven are suspicious of praise.

In his studies, Psychologist Wulf-Uwe Meyer found that kids believe receiving praise from the teacher is a sign they need extra help and encouragement or that they lack ability. The praise is not perceived as a sign that they did well.

Meyer also found that teens "discounted praise to such an extent that they believed it is a teacher's criticism — not praise at all — that really conveys a positive belief in a student's aptitude."

Cognitive scientist Daniel T. Willingham believes that when a teacher praises a child, the teacher is conveying to the student that he has reached the limits of his abilities. On the other hand, criticizing the student conveys that there is room for improvement and that he can do better.

Outside of a very connected and trusting relationship, compliments almost always produce suspicion. Even though the person giving the compliment is trying to do something nice for the other person, the other person cannot wade through the suspicion to get to what the complimentor is really trying to say.

For a compliment not to produce these side effects, there needs to be mutual love and respect and no tension, adversity, or competition between the people. These situations are rare, but they do exist.

Is that what you really want to do ~ create distrust, discomfort, and suspicion? Will this make people more receptive to you or will this create resistance?

Life is hard enough without us going around putting others into a state of resistance to us.

AN IMAGE EXPERT WHO REFUSES TO COMPLIMENT

My client Sarah Shah (sarahshah.com) is an Image and TV Expert. You might think someone in this capacity would rely heavily on compliments. After all, her clients are often in a vulnerable position – half dressed with a stranger who is evaluating her fashion choices. It seems that it would be a situation where it is very important to make the clients feel comfortable and also feel good about what they are doing. Surprisingly (or not), compliments are not part of Sarah's tool bag.

Sarah's take on compliments is a nice summary to the problems with praise and compliments. Here is what Sarah has to say:

> Most people give compliments in an effort to connect with others. Compliments are intended to make people feel good and help them be receptive to you. The opposite actually occurs. People respond to compliments with suspicion. When you give a compliment, the target of the compliment's guard goes up and they just want to know what you want. You actually get a response that is opposite to the one you want.

The most common compliments are about appearance – 'I like your shoes.' 'You look great.' 'That is a nice color on you.' These compliments are the easiest to give because you do not have to know anything about the person or really be paying attention in order to find something to say.

When it comes to how people look, no compliment (or comment of any kind, for that matter) ever works. People already feel silently judged about their physical appearance and dress all the time. The judgment makes them feel bad. Compliments bring that judgment conversation out in the open and make them feel even worse.

Sometimes I accidentally compliment someone when I am working and what a mess it makes! They feel judged, they begin judging themselves, they feel bad, and it is a downward self-esteem spiral.

The worst thing I can do is to compliment someone while working with her in her closet. Once I complimented a client's shoes while we were sorting her closet and all hell broke loose. Suddenly she wanted to know why I liked those shoes. Then she asked if I liked other shoes and somehow she began to doubt all her choices and then she started to doubt everything about herself. Eeek! The compliment opened up the judgment door and allowed in a cascade of head trash. She was already in a vulnerable position, half naked in front of someone who judges image for a living with her questionable fashion choices all around her. The compliment put her over the edge. The only way out of this mess was with acknowledgement (lots and lots of acknowledgement!).

Compliments about how a person looks are even worse between the sexes. Even in business, there is always a sexual undertone in any compliment about appearance.

A man I know got kicked out of a women's networking group because he routinely complimented his female colleagues. He is a kind, respectful and thoughtful person who would never intentionally say something to make another person uncomfortable. Nothing he says is overtly sexual. He says things like 'That dress looks good on you,' 'You have a nice smile,' or 'You look nice today.' He truly thinks he is being nice and making appropriate business small talk. He does not realize that women do not like being around him because his compliments make them feel creepy. When he was asked to leave the group, he was told that it was because he had made inappropriate comments. To this day, he still does not understand that his compliments are the problem.

Even though our intention for complimenting and praising is positive, compliments just do not work the way we have been led to believe they do. Oftentimes, the compliments actually produce a negative effect, an effect that is the complete opposite of what we are trying to accomplish.

Potentially, we could do a complete 180-degree turn here. Something that we have used to define ourselves as good, namely compliments, could now be defined as something that is bad to do to another person. Therefore as a good, kind, caring, and considerate person, maybe you should seriously consider never complimenting again. I have survived quite well for fourteen years without complimenting.

Fortunately, there is another communication tool that will allow you to actually do what you are trying to do with compliments. That tool is acknowledgement.

CHAPTER FIVE

Acknowledgement ~ What It Is And What It Is Not

The dictionary defines acknowledgement as the recognition of the existence, truth, or fact of something.

Compare that to the definition of a compliment: an expression of praise, commendation, or admiration.

Acknowledgement is objective and compliments are subjective. Compliments are judgments and opinions. Nobody wants to be judged. Do you want to be judged? I know that I do not! We have already suffered enough from being judged. The absence of judgment that comes with acknowledgement is such a rarity, such a breath of fresh air!

Existence, truth and fact ~ those are powerful words. An acknowledgement is a statement about the way it is! An acknowledgement is fact based and easily verifiable.

What really motivates people? Is it money, freedom, success? At the deepest level, people are motivated by acknowledgement.

I have a very specific definition for acknowledgement.

Acknowledgement is saying what a person did or the results they produced, without judgment or opinion, and it is delivered with a tone of appreciation, curiosity, or surprise.

The tone implies appreciation. "Wow, you really did something."

The tricky part of acknowledgement is that what you say has to be delivered without your opinion or judgment. If there is any opinion or judgment in your words or in your tone, whatever you say is no longer an acknowledgement. It is a judgment. Your statement is no longer objective. Opinion or judgment makes it subjective.

Another key component to acknowledgement is that it is not about you. This is amazingly hard for people to get at first. It sort of scrambles the brain. Even when I teach this tool to high-level coaches and "people" people, they struggle at first to take themselves out of the equation and to really make it only about the other person. If the communication is in any way about you, then it is not acknowledgement. It is something else.

An easy way to begin to understand this distinction is to understand what acknowledgement is not. It is not complimenting, appreciation, validation, affirmation, thanking, recognition, praise, championing, or cheerleading. There is a time and a place for all of these ~ and they are not acknowledgement. Those things are all about you rather than the other person.

Here is what each of these sounds like:

- ❖ Acknowledgement: "You completed the project on time."
- ❖ Compliment: "The project is wonderful. You are so smart."
- ❖ Appreciation: "I really appreciate your completing this project on time."

❖ Validation: "I see that you have given this project a lot of effort and thought."
❖ Affirmation: "I think you deserve all the credit for this successful project."
❖ Thanking: "Thank you for putting all your time and effort into this project."
❖ Recognition: "It is clear you are a very talented project manager."
❖ Praise: "Awesome job."
❖ Championing: "I told the CEO that you were the right person for this project."
❖ Cheerleading: "I knew you could do it."

Of all these communication tools, the only one that is factual and that puts all of the attention and focus on the other person is the acknowledgement.

All of the other examples are an opinion and can therefore be debated. Are you really a talented project manager or did you just get lucky? Did you really put in a lot of effort and thought, and what is a lot? Do I really appreciate that you got it done or am I trying to butter you up before I ask for something else?

What cannot be debated is that you finished the project on time. It is a fact. It is what you did!

Think of something you recently accomplished and then say to yourself, "I did that!" Notice that you feel good. You also probably feel more confident, more powerful, and more optimistic. Just saying those words - "I did that!" - is tremendously self-affirming. That is the experience you are giving others when you acknowledge them.

Acknowledgement creates a wave of positive energy, optimism, and confidence that a person can ride throughout the day.

When people get acknowledged, they get to see what they really did instead of hearing someone else's opinion about what they did. This is a subtle yet extremely important and powerful distinction.

Oftentimes, they are completely surprised by what they did and they experience a moment of discovery. They might even say something like, "Wow, I really did do that." They also realize that someone is actually paying attention to them. "Wow, somebody noticed!"

With acknowledgement, the sense of satisfaction and accomplishment is being generated internally by that person rather than from an external force trying to convince them. They get to own what they did or the result that they produced. They get to affirm themselves.

An acknowledgement actually produces two acknowledgements. First, you acknowledge them, and then they acknowledge themselves.

Compare that to the feeling created by a compliment, ~ a little unease, a hard time taking it in, counter examples being thought of, and suspicion.

All of these other communication tools require deep trust to be effective. They require the person to take some risk and be open and vulnerable. Acknowledgement does not require this because it creates the experience in them! They experience self-discovery.

SELF-DISCOVERY

I cannot say enough about the importance of self-discovery. When external agendas or judgments are replaced with self-discovery, people flourish. Internal judgments, resistance, discounting, and arguing also disappear.

Giving someone an acknowledgement is like greasing a wheel. It makes everything run a little smoother. It lets people see for themselves where they really are, without any judgment. When there is no judgment, they can make different types of decisions – useful, proactive decisions rather than reactive ones.

Self-discovery versus an external opinion is a lot like the difference between motivation and inspiration. Motivation is an outside force that is trying to get you to do something, usually something you do not want to do. Inspiration is a force that comes from within and invites you to do something you already want to do.

Acknowledgement allows people to look at their lives from a different perspective, namely the perspective of what they are doing that is working and what they are doing that is not working. This perspective tends to create positivity and optimism. From this perspective, people believe more in themselves and see themselves as more capable, competent, and confident. Clearly, this is a very different result than that produced by most people's habitual perspective of judgment.

A new perspective can create the freedom for us to experience different thoughts, expectations, behaviors and, ultimately, different results.

In his TEDxBloomington talk, Shawn Achor says, "It is not necessarily the reality that shapes us, but the lens through which your brain views the world that shapes your reality. If we can change the lens, not only can we change your happiness, we can change every single education and business outcome at the same time."

This is exactly what acknowledgement does. It changes your lens to one of positivity, capability, success, and accomplishment.

Achor also tells us that when the brain is in a positive state, it is 31% more productive than a brain in a neutral, negative, or stress state. Your brain in a positive state provides you with the happiness advantage, where you have increased intelligence, creativity, and energy.

ACKNOWLEDGEMENT PRODUCES THE DESIRED RESULTS

One of the fascinating things about acknowledgement is that it successfully produces the results that the other communication tools are trying – but usually failing - to accomplish.

A person who has been acknowledged does feel appreciated, validated, and recognized. And they get to praise themselves, which is way more meaningful than external praise can ever be. They get to be their own champion and cheerleader. This builds self-confidence, self-worth, self-esteem, and trust in their own capability.

Feelings of appreciation and validation are built into every acknowledgement and in such a way that it is clear to the receiver that it is about them and what they did, not about the person delivering the acknowledgement.

Furthermore, acknowledgement creates action-ability. There is a clear path in front of the person being acknowledged of what they should repeat. They know what should be done the next time in order to produce the desired result.

ACKNOWLEDGEMENT DELIVERS ATTENTION

Acknowledgement is also a very effective tool for delivering attention.

Your attention is the most precious and powerful gift you can give another and as I have already mentioned, attention is in short supply. Plus, in a sea of "all about me", when we actually make it about them, it stands out and makes an impact!

When you give an acknowledgement, it literally might be the only time in a person's week where it is all about them, where they are receiving full attention.

When you acknowledge people, what is the message? The message is: WOW, you are really paying attention to them. When you pay enough attention to find something to acknowledge someone for, and then you acknowledge him or her, that person feels the attention. People feel totally validated. They experience being seen, heard, and that you get them, and that you are really present.

Acknowledgement makes people realize that someone is actually paying attention to them (for a change). "Wow, somebody noticed!"

Think about what happens on playgrounds all the time. The kid keeps saying, "Watch this, mom!" or "Watch me, daddy!" Over and over, they ask to be watched. The kids want attention. They want to know that they are being watched. This makes them feel reassured, valued, and important.

Adults are no different (they are just taller kids). They want to be noticed too. Acknowledgement shows that we have been watching. We have been paying attention, and it is tremendously reassuring.

Acknowledgement also delivers your belief in them, your belief in their being, your belief in their capability, and your belief in their magnificence. There is nothing you can do to be a stronger wind in someone's sail than to acknowledge them.

ACKNOWLEDGEMENT AND VITALITY

Learning to consistently acknowledge instead of complimenting, praising, and appreciating will probably take some work on your part.

An easy way to get yourself inspired to do this work is to watch the vitality and aliveness in the other person. The easiest way to do this is to pay attention to their eyes.

You know the old saying that the eyes are the window to the soul. Our eyes are a great indicator about what is going on with us. We can see vitality – or the lack of vitality - in people's eyes.

Acknowledgement lights people up (the lights in the back of their eyes turn on). You can see this when you watch. They get brighter. This means that their vitality and aliveness have increased.

On the other hand, the light in people's eyes almost always dims when they are complimented, praised, or appreciated. If you watch, you can actually see this. Their vitality and aliveness goes down.

Most people have not learned how to pay attention to this distinction. However, it is quite easy to learn how to do this, and once you start paying attention to this, you will be amazed by what you see.

So much of what people do to each other turns down the lights, which means that it negatively impacts the quality of their life.

Acknowledgement consistently and reliably turns up the lights! This means that when we acknowledge, we are positively contributing to the quality of their life!

This is why I do not compliment, praise, or appreciate any more. I watch the lights, the vitality, and I see what happens. I have zero interest in turning down people's lights. I have massive interest in turning up people's lights and that is why I acknowledge.

It is really quite simple. When people feel truly acknowledged, they light up. When people do not feel acknowledged, they do not light up.

RESISTANCE AND RECEPTIVITY

In my fourteen years of using this tool, and seven years of teaching it to people, I have rarely seen compliments, praise, or appreciation light up the receiver. The vast majority of the time, it actually takes their lights out, closes them down, and creates resistance.

At any given time, a person can be in one of two states: resistance or receptivity. There is no middle ground here. You are either in a state of receptivity or a state of resistance.

Obviously, when resistance is present, things get harder, performance decreases, expectations take a downward turn, self-belief and self-confidence decrease, and willingness decreases. Positive change, inspiration, and growth cannot happen in the face of resistance.

Start observing people and their interactions. You will soon notice that most people are really good at putting other people into a state of resistance. They are not doing this on purpose. They usually do not even know they are doing it. They simply do not know any better (after all, we have been taught that compliments, praise, and appreciation work). Nonetheless, that is what they are doing over and over and over. Then they wonder why life is so hard.

When someone lights up, they are curious and receptive. When someone does not light up, they are resistant and closed off. Acknowledgement lights people up and, consequently, acknowledgement creates receptivity.

Because of this, acknowledgement makes your life better while making other people's lives better. It is truly a win-win tool!

CHAPTER SIX

How To Acknowledge

Author and seminary professor Steve Brown famously said, "Anything worth doing is worth doing poorly until you learn to do it well."

At first, acknowledgement might be awkward and uncomfortable. You will probably make it harder than it really is.

Acknowledgement will also probably just *feel* different and unfamiliar to you when you deliver it. You are used to feeling self-expressed, heartfelt, eloquent, and creative when you compliment and, at first, acknowledgement will not feel that way.

Furthermore, any time we change a habit, in this case the habit of complimenting, the new behavior will usually feel awkward, unnatural, or unfamiliar.

I have seen this over and over when I teach acknowledgement. Your head will make up all sorts of stuff because acknowledgement is unfamiliar. Your head will tell you that acknowledgement is cold, impersonal, not heartfelt, uncaring, and even stupid.

Kevin, the owner of an aviation design and photography company, attended a workshop where I taught acknowledgement. He said, "It is kind of funny when you sit there in class telling a complete stranger something they already know. Well at least that was how

55

I looked at it. But then as I was rotating around the room and interacting with other people it clicked. Acknowledging them became important to everyone. It was like giving a person a gold star. Watching people light up was incredible. After the class it was hard for me to think that everything I have been doing at work was garbage."

Kevin's experience is very common because we are used to complimenting, praising, and appreciating. We are so used to it that when we do anything else, it feels strange.

If you try to understand acknowledgement and figure it out in your head, you will not succeed. The best thing to do is just go out and experience the power of acknowledgement. Give some acknowledgements and witness the impact that it has on the other person. When you do that, your heart is going to get it. Your heart will comprehend the difference that acknowledgement makes! Sometimes you can hear the difference between acknowledgements and compliments; other times, it can be very subtle where you just feel the difference.

Acknowledgement makes a difference in people's lives and is one of the kindest things we can ever do for another person.

You have a choice. Do you want to feel good about yourself or do you want others to feel great about themselves?

ACKNOWLEDGEMENT IS
WHAT THEY ACTUALLY DID

An acknowledgement is simply a statement of what the other person did, or the result that they produced, without judgment (good or bad) or opinion, delivered with a tone of appreciation, curiosity, or surprise.

"You got a new client!" "You ate your asparagus!" "You arrived on time!" "You made five phone calls!" "You exercised today!" "You responded to my email!" "You matched your jewelry to your blouse!" "You included everyone in the conversation today!" "You hit the fairway on 16 of 18 drives!" "You brushed your teeth!"

If any of the above seems trite or even demeaning, that simply means you are trying to figure out acknowledgement with your head. Acknowledgement is a heart thing. A person hearing any of these will experience a surge of positive energy and will feel good about him or herself.

It also means you are making it more about you, and what you think and feel, than about the other person. The only thing that matters is the impact the acknowledgement has on the receiver.

Again, this is new stuff and will be unfamiliar, unnatural, or even counterintuitive. Acknowledgement is an experiential thing. You have to give acknowledgements in order to understand acknowledgement! There is no other way.

Each one of the above examples is a verifiable fact. It is something they did or a result they produced. They can say, "Yes, I did!"

Notice what is not in these examples ~ my opinion or judgment. Pure acknowledgement is simply what happened or what result was produced.

"That is great ~ you got a new client!" Now my opinion is involved. It is my opinion that it is great that you got a new client.

This is a significant shift in energy, content, and attention. Now part of the content is about me, "in my opinion," and part of the attention and energy is on me, as well. I have made a judgment about you.

An acknowledgement of behavior over time really shows that you are paying attention. "You washed the dishes every day this week!" This tells the other person that you have been paying attention and noticing what he or she was up to.

MAKE IT SPECIFIC

An acknowledgement needs to be specific. What did someone do? What exactly happened? What result was produced? Acknowledgements must be specific in order to be effective.

If I tell someone, "You did it. You finished!" right after they cross the finish line, they will know what I am talking about. If I say the same thing to them a week later, "You finished!" they will want to know what they finished: lunch, the laundry, a book??? In order to create value, I need to be specific, "You finished the race!"

"Shelly, you were helpful" is not an acknowledgement. Neither is, "Shelly, you provided clarity." Neither of those is specific. They are vague. The cure for vagueness is to ask yourself, "What did Shelly actually do that would make me say that she was helpful or provided clarity?" Oh, she answered my question, which I found to be helpful and which provided me with clarity. So, the acknowledgement is, "Shelly, you answered my question!"

An acknowledgement must be about something people did or a result they produced. It is about the facts.

Recently, a colleague of mine invited me to teach her coaching students about the tool of acknowledgement. After I explained what acknowledgement was and gave them a few examples, I asked them if they wanted to give it a try.

The first person to try her hand at acknowledgement said to me, "You are very inclusive."

I told her, "That is a compliment, not an acknowledgement."

She said, "Oh, I know, that was not about something you did."

I responded, "That is right. That is the story you made up about something I did rather than what I actually did. Just say the part that I did."

She then said, "You included everyone in the conversation today!"

I told her, "I feel acknowledged by that. That is exactly what I did."

Say those two sentences out loud: "You are very inclusive." "You included everyone in the conversation today." Notice how different they feel. The former has a judgment or opinion while the latter is a statement of fact.

SOMETHING THAT IS COMPLETED

You cannot acknowledge something that people are doing in the moment, or something that they plan to do. An acknowledgement has to be about something that is done. It needs to be complete.

Feel the difference between, "You are working on your taxes." And, "You worked on your taxes yesterday." Notice how there is more satisfaction, validation, and energy with something that is done versus something that is still in process. Even if the tax project is not completed, yesterday's work is completed.

Also, you cannot really acknowledge what someone did not do. "You did not exercise. You did not eat right." You cannot own a "not."

You have to turn that into what they did. For example, you could acknowledge not exercising and not eating right by saying, "You just told me all the stuff that you did not do!" That is an acknowledgement. That is what they did. Or "You avoided exercising yesterday!" That is something they did; they avoided.

MAKE IT SHORT

The shorter an acknowledgement, the more impact it has. New acknowledgers usually make their acknowledgements too long.

Ultimately, what acknowledgement does is it puts someone's attention on something specific. So the more complex you make it, the less attention they can put on the acknowledgement because their attention goes to processing what it all means.

Compare the impact of "You turned in your report on time" vs. "You turned in your 25-page report on the new market variables and how that could potentially impact our market share and you turned it in within the specified time frame."

In the second example, you get lost and bored and the power of the acknowledgement gets diluted. The acknowledgement is just too long to be effective.

ONE THING AT A TIME

New acknowledgers also tend to combine several specific things into one acknowledgement. "You arrived on time, brought the papers to sign, brought an extra pen, and picked a convenient place to meet!"

This all kind of blurs together and actually creates the experience of not being acknowledged.

Compare that with, "You arrived on time!" Pause. "You brought the papers to sign!" Pause. "You brought an extra pen!" Pause "You picked a convenient place to meet!" The other person gets to say, "Yes, I did!" four separate times.

Say one acknowledgement and let it land! Then say another and let it land!

The best acknowledgements are short, simple, specific, and about only one thing.

JUST LISTEN

People will always tell you what they want to be acknowledged for. But, you have to be paying attention to hear it. If you are busy trying to find or compose a compliment, you will never hear it when they tell you what they want to be acknowledged for.

The easiest way to acknowledge people is to actually listen to them and then repeat back to them what they just said with a tone of genuine appreciation, wonder, curiosity, or surprise.

This requires that you let go of your preconceived notions of the way a conversation is supposed to go. Sometimes you just need to act like a parrot and repeat back to them what they just said.

> Dad: "What did you do at school today?"
> Son: "I played soccer at recess and I finished reading my book."
> Dad: "You played soccer today!"
> Son (inside his own head): "Yes, I did!"
> Dad: "You finished your book!"
> Son (inside his own head): "Yes, I did!"

You do not need to find something huge and dramatic to acknowledge. Even the acknowledgement of seemingly mundane things will cause people to feel good about themselves. What you acknowledge does not have to be big; it just has to be what they did or a result they produced.

LEAVE YOURSELF OUT OF IT

The hardest part about acknowledgement is taking yourself out of it. As soon as the word "I" shows up, then it is no longer about them; it is about you. Leave yourself completely out of the equation. This can be challenging because of what we are used to doing.

"You sent me the information, which allowed me to catch up on what I had missed."

In this example, it is a good start, then "I" comes in, and it becomes about me. "I was able to catch up."

The acknowledgement is simply, "You sent me the information!" That is what the other person did.

You might be thinking, "But wait, there is an 'I' (me) in 'You sent me the information." There is, but it is not about me. It is about what you did. You sent the information to me. That is a fact. That is what you did.

Imagine someone picks you up at the airport. The acknowledgement would be, "You picked me up!" It would sound awkward or unclear without the "me" in the sentence. "You picked up!" What exactly did you pick up?

"I" can never be in an acknowledgement. "Me" can. And, if you can leave out the "me" and the sentence still makes sense, then even better. "You sent me the information" makes just as much sense without the "me." "You sent the information!"

An acknowledgement does not need to be explained. An explanation waters down the acknowledgement and it also becomes more about you and your understanding and clarity.

Just say what they did. They get it! It is only your need to be understood that makes you want to explain it. People are smart and perceptive and they get it. Explaining takes away from the power. Reasons are about you, not them. If it is about something they did or a result they got, they already know!

Compare: "You showed us a simpler way to do this which was really important because we were confused and were not really grasping the concept." Or, "You showed us a simpler way!"

The acknowledgement speaks directly to them. It is about the person being acknowledged, not about the acknowledger.

NO ADJECTIVES AND MODIFIERS

Another big challenge people have in learning how to acknowledge is to keep their opinions and judgments out of it. Just one little word can sabotage an acknowledgement and turn it into something else ~ a judgment.

Feel the difference between "You spoke your mind!" and "You spoke your mind clearly!"

There is a different energy between the two examples. "You spoke your mind" probably makes you feel good. "You spoke your mind clearly" probably makes you feel a little deflated. It ends on a down note because you are now being judged once again.

It is subtle but in the second example, some of the attention now goes to me. I now have an opinion about whether you spoke clearly or not. This puts me in a position of power. I get to decide. I get to be the judge.

And really, who is looking for more opportunities to feel judged? We have all experienced more than enough of that already.

If you feel judged, you cannot hear what the other person intended for you to hear. You just hear the judgment. It is almost impossible to sort through the judgment to get to what was useful.

As soon as modifiers and descriptors enter into your acknowledgement, you are no longer acknowledging – you are judging.

"I spoke too quietly." Can you feel the judgment in that, the self-beating and self-judgment?

Compare that to, "I spoke quietly." That is just a statement of the fact.

Compare the feeling between "You hit the ball hard" and "You hit the ball!" One little word (in this case, "hard") can undercut an acknowledgement and suck the power out of it.

All you need to do is acknowledge the hitting of the ball. They will fill in the details for themselves in the way that works best for them. Your acknowledgement gives them the opportunity to create their own appropriate meaning to this event.

ACKNOWLEDGE INDIVIDUALS
NOT GROUPS

Group acknowledgements are not as powerful as individual acknowledgements.

In a group acknowledgement, people will often make up in their minds that you are not talking to them but are talking to everyone else or someone else specifically in the group. Consequently, individual actions and results are way more powerful to acknowledge.

Compare "You all showed up on time!" to "Bob, you showed up on time!" The plural just does not produce much feeling. The singular produces, "Yes, I did!" Bob can now own the result that he produced.

TURN COMPLIMENTS INTO
ACKNOWLEDGEMENT

If you find yourself trying to acknowledge and end up complimenting instead, that is okay because you can turn the compliment into an acknowledgement.

The way to do that is to ask yourself, "What did they do that makes me say that?" You are looking for what they did or the results they produced that caused you to deliver the compliment in the first place.

"You look nice" ~ oh, right, what did she do that makes me say that? I see that she got a hair cut.

So with a slight adjustment, the compliment can become an acknowledgement. "You got a hair cut!" That is the acknowledgement. That is the fact about what actually happened and it lands differently.

Comments on physical characteristics are not acknowledgements. Even if it were something they had control over, like having big biceps, you would have to acknowledge what they did to get those biceps. "You have lifted weights three times a week for five years!"

TONE MATTERS

Part of the definition of acknowledgement is that it is said with a tone of appreciation, curiosity, or surprise.

You want the tone to have a little energy with it. You want to give the person some energy with your acknowledgement.

You tone implies, "Wow! That is cool, fascinating, or noteworthy." In order to generate that kind of tone, you want to look at things through curious eyes. You cannot generate that kind of tone if you are judging, bored, already know it all, or are not really paying attention to them.

If your tone is flat, neutral, or disinterested, they will either not feel acknowledged at all or else the acknowledgement will have far less impact.

Think about a recent accomplishment and say, "I did that!" with some energy and appreciation. Then say the same thing but with a bored detached tone. Notice the difference. Acknowledgement is more than just the words. It is also the spirit behind the words.

One of the amazing things about acknowledgement is that there is praise and appreciation within every acknowledgement. But, the praise and appreciation are not voiced. They are in the tone. They are there energetically and intentionally. This allows the person being acknowledged to experience self-discovery and generate that praise and appreciation within themselves. When these things are internally generated, it creates such a different experience than when they are externally forced on someone.

STRATEGIC PRAISE

Also, once you become skilled in acknowledgement, then you can start to strategically use a little praise after the acknowledgement.

When you do this, it is essential to lead with the acknowledgement. Otherwise, they will get stuck in praise and will not hear the acknowledgement. Also, if you lead with praise, then it becomes about you and your judgment and opinion.

When doing this, leave a significant gap between the two so that the acknowledgement can land.

"You washed the dishes!" ... pause . . . wait . . . wait some more ... wait ... okay the acknowledgement has landed. Now you can praise. "You rock!" "Good job!" "Way to go!" ~ or some other praise expression.

One way to create a hypnotic trance is to say a few facts and then follow up with something that is not a fact. "You are sitting in the chair" (fact). "You hear the music in the background" (fact). And, "You are beginning to relax" (not a fact).

The brain gets on a roll of dealing with facts and it then accepts the non-fact as a fact, too.

That is basically the same way that praise after an acknowledgement works. We recognize the factualness of the acknowledgement. "Yes, I did that!" So then when we hear the praise, we believe that the praise is true, too. "Yes, I do rock!"

The praise lands in a way that it never would on its own.

However, do not get carried away with praise. You do not need the praise. Acknowledgements – on their own – are the most powerful communication tool I know of!

To start with, do not use acknowledgement and praise together. Just acknowledge for now.

ACKNOWLEDGEMENT DOES NOT
REQUIRE A RESPONSE

Acknowledgement does not require any response. The person does not need to say "Thank you." If you are sitting there waiting for a response to your acknowledgement, then your attention is on you. The only valid reason to acknowledge is . . . because you can. If it is ever about you, if it is self-serving, or if you are trying to get something or manipulate, it is no longer acknowledgement.

EVEN THE "EXPERTS" DO NOT
HAVE THIS TOOL

Part of the reason I wrote this book is that so few coaches (and other people whose job it is to help people experience positive change and growth) have this amazing tool. They are using compliments and praise even though those communication tools do not really work. Those tools do not light people up, inspire them, validate them, or support them in figuring out what to do next.

Not too long ago Diana Nyad was being interviewed on the *Today Show*. Diana was being interviewed because at the age of sixty-one, she attempted to swim from Cuba to the Florida Keys without a shark cage. This was a big endeavor, one that no one of any age has completed.

On her blog, Diana tells of an interaction she had in the green room before her interview. Diana spoke with a well-known coach who is often a contributor on the *Today Show*.

Here is some of what this famous coach had to say: "I appreciate what you did and how you did it. You went about planning the swim as safely as you could, not recklessly. You were clear about what you wanted to do and you did your best. What more can you ask of yourself? Most things do not work out for most of us — the big things — so the way we handle things is all we have. And you handle things beautifully."

To the untrained eye, what she said might look like a bunch of acknowledgement. It is not!

Read that again and notice how you feel. There is not an ounce of real validation there. There is nothing that is a true acknowledgment ~ specifically what Diana did. There is not one thing where Diana can say, "Yes, I did!" and experience true satisfaction. There is not one single acknowledgement in what the coach said.

Instead, the whole thing is full of judgment and opinion. Ultimately, it is all about the coach rather than Diana, even though it is supposed to be about Diana, the woman who just did something amazing by attempting to swim from Cuba to the Florida Keys at the age of sixty-one.

Now I am not picking on this famous coach. I am just pointing out that very few people know how to use this amazing tool of acknowledgement. Consequently, people are not doing as good a job as they could if they simply adopted this one tool.

This coach is doing what she knows. She is simply working with tools that are not very effective.

Can we turn what she said into acknowledgement? Of course we can!

I followed Diana's swim from Cuba on Facebook, her Blog, and Twitter. However, I do not know her and have never spoken to her. That does not mean that I cannot acknowledge her.

Diana,
You planned a safe swim! ("not reckless" is a judgment)
You kept yourself safe on your swim! (fact)
You swam for thirty hours! ("did your best" is a judgment. The only one who knows if she did her best is Diana.)
You assembled a support team of experts! (fact)
You spoke to reporters and your fans afterward! ("handled things beautifully" is a judgment)
You inspired thousands of people! (fact)
You kept us updated on your progress on your blog! (fact)

Let me get on my soapbox for a minute. Why don't more coaches (and other people whose job it is to support people and assist them to create positive change and growth) use this amazing tool?

Even the vast majority of coaches think it is supposed to be about them and that the "client" needs them to give their opinion and approval. That is, in my opinion, just plain disrespectful. And in fact, it sends the message, "I know what is better for you than you know for yourself." Isn't coaching supposed to lift up and empower? How does that happen when it is about the coaches' opinions, judgments, and approval?

Acknowledgement clears up all of these problems. Acknowledgement is all about them, not about us. It provides accurate feedback on what they have done or the result that was produced. People very seldom get true feedback. They get the story, along with the judgment about what they did. When people know what they actually did, they can organize around that fact and either do more of the same or do something different and more appropriate. People cannot organize around a story. Acknowledgement is information that people can actually use!

REALLY LISTENING

A client of mine, Eric Lejeune (strideleadership.com), is a Personal Leadership Strategist. He shares his experience with using acknowledgement.

> The tool of acknowledgement has been a total game changer. When I first learned how to really acknowledge someone, it was a real eye opener on how little attention I truly paid to other people when talking to them. I mean, I thought I listened to others. If you asked me what they said, I could repeat it back to you (most of the time). But being able to acknowledge someone requires that you not only hear but also listen on another level. You have to really listen to people in order to acknowledge an action or result that they achieved. For me, learning how to truly acknowledge someone also taught me how to truly listen.

Now that I am no longer a novice at the acknowledgement game, I can say that it has become something I use not just to get what I want, but a tool that I use just because I can. When you can see a physical difference in the response of someone by just saying a few words, it becomes hard not to do so. It has become fun to watch people gain a sudden burst of energy or excitement that they are not even conscious about. I have found that leaving people feeling appreciated and listened to makes the world a better place for all of us and comes back to me in much bigger ways.

START ACKNOWLEDGING NOW

Please do not take my word for how powerful acknowledgement is. Go out in the laboratory, i.e., the world, and experiment. See what results you can produce through the use of acknowledgement.

Quit trying to figure out acknowledgement. Dive in and start delivering acknowledgements. That is how you will learn!

Be patient with yourself. The skill of acknowledgement is simple, yet so tricky. The principle is straightforward but challenging to apply. To become skillful in acknowledgement requires practice, a lot of practice.

The work is worth it because acknowledgement is so powerful.

Have you ever taught a child to throw a baseball? Learning acknowledgement is like a kid learning to throw. The first 100 throws do not go anywhere near the mitt. In fact, they go everywhere but straight to the glove. They go over your head, to the side, straight into the ground, all over the place. This is just what it takes to learn how to make an accurate throw.

As the teacher, what do you do? No matter where the ball goes, you encourage them to keep trying. You are willing to tolerate all of the missed throws because that is part of the learning curve of how to throw a baseball.

Learning any new skill requires us to tolerate our own learning curve. As adults, we are usually not very good at this. Even when it is something new, we want to do it well the first time we attempt it. That is probably not going to happen with acknowledgement.

So just get out there and try. It is OK if your acknowledgement is not perfect the first time. Just promise me you will tolerate your learning curve and keep at it.

YOUR ASSIGNMENT

If you choose to accept it, your mission is to deliver ten acknowledgements a day for the rest of your life! In order for acknowledgement to be natural, you need to acknowledge a lot!

CHAPTER SEVEN

Acknowledgement As Feedback

I used to be a commercial fisherman in Alaska (It was a lot like the show *Deadliest Catch* on the Discovery Channel, although not in front of a TV camera). That experience gave me a deep understanding of the necessity of feedback and course correction.

Successful navigation of the boat required almost constant course correction. Whether it was the autopilot or manually steering, we were constantly taking in feedback and readjusting our course.

Processing this feedback and making the subsequent course corrections allowed us to go where we wanted to go instead of where the tides, winds, and currents would take us.

People need that same type of course correction in their lives. In fact, peak performance is impossible without feedback. Yet most people do not receive nearly enough meaningful feedback.

Noted leadership trainer Ken Blanchard said, "Feedback is the breakfast of champions."

Feedback allows us to see where we are, where we are headed and to course correct when need be. If we do not know how we are doing or where we are headed, then how can we possibly know what to do next? English composer and conductor Sir Peter Maxwell Davies said,

"If you don't get feedback . . . you're going to be working in a vacuum."

Acknowledgement provides that feedback. When you are acknowledged, you get to hear what you did that worked or what you did that did not work. Based on that feedback, you can do more of the same, or you can adjust and do something different.

ACKNOWLEDGING WHAT DID NOT WORK

Up to this point in the book, we have been talking about acknowledging what the person did that worked.

However, there is also tremendous value in acknowledging what did not work.

This kind of acknowledgement is feedback that the person is off course and needs to do something different to get back on course.

"You were late." "You turned in incomplete homework." "You offended the client." "You broke your promise." These are statements of fact about what you did or the result that you produced. This feedback delivered without judgment or opinion can allow you to easily course correct from something that does not work to something that does.

In most organizations, and in most of our culture, for that matter, this is not the kind of feedback that people use. In most situations when people give feedback, it is really their opinion, judgment, or suggestion on how things should be done differently. It is not true feedback and certainly in no way, shape, or form is it acknowledgement.

The rules for acknowledging something that did not work are the same as acknowledging something that did work. The acknowledgement is something they did or a result they produced, delivered with a tone of curiosity, appreciation, or surprise (without opinion or judgment).

This is where tone and intention are so important. These two factors will make or break your acknowledgement. Once you have a tone of judgment or opinion, you are no longer acknowledging. You are judging.

Contrast "You were late" with a tone that implies, "You are bad - you idiot" with "You were late," stated simply as a statement of fact. Even better, state it with a tone of curiosity or appreciation of their accomplishment. And yes, being late is an accomplishment. What did they have to do in order to be late? How did they have to run their life in order to produce that result? Late is a result that they produced and therefore is an accomplishment.

These two examples are worlds apart in the impact they have. The former provides judgment and all the negative consequences that come with that. It is an opportunity for you to grind your axe and to be right! This immediately puts the person in a defensive position and creates resistance. Nobody enjoys being judged!

The latter provides objective feedback (rather than your subjective judgment or opinion), which allows the person to see the results of his or her behavior. Because it is just a statement of the facts, there is nothing to argue with. The facts are the facts - end of sentence - end of discussion. This creates acceptance, which allows the receiver of the acknowledgement to accept rather than defend his or her results or behavior. Without the pressure of having to defend, it becomes much easier to influence or modify future performance.

Along the same line of reasoning, someone who can also acknowledge what did not work without judging creates a safer environment where others don't have to fear "getting in trouble" when mistakes are made. They can count on the facts being dealt with, rather than a reaction to a judgment.

FREEDOM TO LET GO

The absence of judgment in acknowledgement makes it really easy to let go of feeling bad about something you did. Think of something you are feeling bad about or are having problems letting go of. Out loud, acknowledge yourself for what you did or the result you produced ~ remember, just the facts without judgment or opinion. Then see what happens. Chances are you will experience relief and some peace of mind. The acknowledgement helped you to let go. This, of course, helps you to move forward.

This is the same experience you create for others when you acknowledge what they did that did not work. It creates freedom!

THE ONLY WAY TO MISUSE ACKNOWLEDGEMENT

The only way the tool of acknowledgement can be misused is to pretend that you are acknowledging (providing objective feedback) when in reality you are judging.

If you feel judgment, you will convey a tone of judgment and the person will experience being judged. Do not pretend to be acknowledging when you are judging. Be honest in your communication and do not sully the tool of acknowledgement.

Otherwise, you can create a distrust of the acknowledgement process with those you want to use it with. People will not want to take part in the process if it is being misused to further your agenda or to punish.

I have seen and experienced the tool of acknowledgement being misused this way and it is not pretty. Please do not do this!

Remember, people should always feel lighter and better after acknowledgement. This is true even after an acknowledgement of something that did not work. If they do not, then you were not acknowledging.

If you cannot deliver a "negative" with appreciation or curiosity, then it is not acknowledgement. It is "being right" so call it what it is!

Of course, this is quite easy to say and much more challenging to do. You must first let go of your upset and move yourself into a state of curiosity, surprise, or appreciation. You absolutely must remove all judgment.

When you deliver feedback like, "You are late" in the back of your mind there needs to be something like: "Wow, I wonder how you did that (with genuine curiosity)? What did it actually take for you to be late?" or an appreciation of how you accomplished the feat of being late.

Delivering "negative" feedback as a genuine acknowledgement takes at least three things: practice, getting your attention off of yourself and on to the other person, and a strong desire to communicate in an effective way that contributes to the other person.

Many managers and leaders have been taught the feedback sandwich technique (because they lack the skill of acknowledgement). The general idea is that if you need to give people "constructive criticism" or correction, you stick it between two pieces of positive feedback. Well, this is flat out stupid. People know what you are up to. Instead of hearing any of the positive, they only hear the negative. The management consultant that invented the feedback sandwich should be shot. The feedback sandwich does more harm than good. (More on this in chapter 10.)

In his book, *Quiet Leadership*, David Rock said (about the feedback sandwich), "I propose this is just a manipulative way to disguise that we are going to talk about what people did wrong."

Acknowledgement eliminates the need for this type of manipulation. Acknowledgement is professional feedback, not management (read amateur feedback), not your opinion, not what you think about the actions, but what actually happened. "John, you were late. Susie you were on time."

PROFESSIONAL FEEDBACK

I had a manager in my class. Let's call her Deb. She had an employee who was always late (usually by about 15 minutes). Deb had tried everything she knew how to try in order to address the employee's lateness, but nothing seemed to get through and no improvement was made.

After we discussed the skill of acknowledgement, Deb decided this would be a great situation to test out acknowledgement. So, following the same instructions that I have given you, Deb began to acknowledge.

Each time the employee was late, she would go to her office and with a neutral or appreciative tone say, "Nancy, you were late today." Nothing else ~ no request for an explanation, no threats, no implied judgment, and no making Nancy wrong. If Nancy was on time to work, Deb would go and acknowledge her for that, simply saying, "Nancy, you were on time today." Deb used no praise, no explanation, and no requests to do it again tomorrow.

After about two weeks, an amazing thing happened. Nancy started arriving on time almost all of the time.

Feedback about something that did not work, given in the pure acknowledgement form where there is no judgment or opinion, is easy to take in. Because it is light in nature, it allows us to learn and course correct. We do not have to waste all of our resources on defending, justifying, sharing the blame, wallowing in self-pity, and other useless pursuits.

Instead of acknowledgement, people use threats, judgment, and make-wrong. That is what Deb had been trying, to no avail. These things do not work even though oftentimes they are all that people know how to do. They create resistance, which actually makes it more difficult for a person to change, course correct, or improve.

A colleague of mine, who holds a director-level position at the University of Houston, recently told me a similar story. A friend of his at work, who is a supervisor, was venting to him that she had an employee, John, who was always late to meetings. As his supervisor, she had tried everything she knew to do in order to try and correct the behavior. Nothing had worked.

My colleague, who had taken several of our leadership trainings and learned the skill of acknowledgement, suggested that she try acknowledgement. He instructed her that the next time John came in late to a meeting to just say matter of factly, and without judgment, "John you are ____ minutes late". He also instructed her not to say or do anything else ~ don't be judgmental, don't make a threat, and don't have any additional commentary about it.

Three weeks later, the supervisor went into my friend's office and said, "You are a genius. I did what you told me to do and within a couple of meetings John started arriving on time, and he continues to be on time."

The great thing about this story is that the supervisor had all of about five minutes of instruction in how to use acknowledgement. This was enough for her to get fast satisfactory results. Acknowledgement can be that simple and that powerful!

When feedback is delivered without judgment or opinion, the other person can accept it, they can work with it, and they can own the results. The major problem with almost all feedback is that it is delivered with judgment. Once the receiver feels and hears that judgment, it is difficult for them to "hear" anything else. Any sort of judgment immediately puts most people into a state of defensiveness, and rightly so. Consequently, feedback delivered with judgment almost never gets heard, even if it is accurate. (Hearing feedback through judgment requires a maturity that very few people possess).

If the feedback is, first of all, not even heard, and then secondly, the person is busy reeling from and distracted by the judgment, it becomes virtually impossible for the person to take in the feedback and make an adjustment based on it.

Additionally, judgment and opinion will almost always create resistance in the other person. So even if the person wants to improve, now we have put him or her in a situation where that person has to overcome that resistance to even start to make an improvement.

I love to say, "People do not resist getting better; they resist the judgment that they are not good enough!"

Acknowledgement, by definition, has an absence of judgment. Just the simple fact that there is no judgment being expressed has the acknowledgement show up in the receiver's experience as belief in them and in their abilities and capabilities. Acknowledgement expresses your belief in them and in their ability to course correct and to do what works in place of what does not work.

When people do not feel judged, they feel accepted. Acceptance feels like belief. When someone feels as if you believe in him or her, they almost automatically believe in themselves more. Conversely, when you judge them, they believe in themselves less.

Think about all the stories you have heard about kids rising up out of extreme conditions of need or poverty. All of these stories have the same common theme. Someone (a coach, a teacher, a relative, a sibling, or a mentor) somewhere along the line believed in them.

When you believe in someone, it is absolutely a gift you are giving. When you put your belief in someone, it is like rocket fuel for that person's life.

When you acknowledge someone, you are putting your belief straight into that individual. There is no more direct route.

You are holding them as more capable than they hold themselves and that is a very powerful thing to do.

I have seen it over and over in my years of working with this tool. Even though I have called acknowledgement the invisible language of results, it is really more like rocket fuel for the human spirit and for achievement.

I guarantee that when you acknowledge someone enough, he or she will take inspired action! The amount of acknowledgement needed for this varies from person to person and situation to situation. Generally, the less confident and the more beat down a person is, the more acknowledgement he or she will need to get to the position of being able to take inspired action.

On the other hand, judgment shows up as not believing in them. Implied badness or wrongness cannot coexist with belief in them and their ability to perform at a high level.

A friend's seventeen-year-old son got his driver's license taken away for reckless driving. One parent used acknowledgement and the other did not. Not surprisingly, the two parents created very different impacts on their son and on their relationship with their son.

The parent who did not use acknowledgement created distance and put a strain on the relationship. Ultimately, the message that got delivered was, "You really messed up. What is wrong with you?" The son was left with the feeling that this parent had no belief in him and thought that he was an idiot.

The other parent simply acknowledged, "You lost your driver's license" which was a statement of what actually happened. The son was able to own this result. "Yes, that is what I did." And that was the end of the conversation. They did not need to go anywhere else with this because the son had owned the result he produced. Once he owned the result, he could course correct. This conveyed belief in the son and in his ability to handle the situation.

Remember, if you have any agenda except to uplift and inspire the other person, then whatever you say is not acknowledgement.

Feedback, whether positive or negative, given as acknowledgement can be heard and acted upon.

CHAPTER EIGHT

Self-Acknowledgement

If you are not receiving enough acknowledgement, you have three choices. You can sit around and wait for someone else to acknowledge you. You can ask for what you want to be acknowledged for and train others to acknowledge you, or you can acknowledge yourself.

I will let you in on a little-known secret. Did you know that it is actually legal to say positive things to yourself? There is no law prohibiting you from speaking kindly to yourself. Seriously, it is okay to do that. Positive self-talk is allowed.

Just a little self-acknowledgement can have substantial beneficial effects on how you feel about yourself.

It is similar to when it rains in the desert. All of a sudden, there are little flowers everywhere. Self-acknowledgement causes feelings of well-being, self-confidence, optimism, happiness, and self-worth to bloom. Plus, it gives you a jolt of energy and enthusiasm.

Once you create the habit of self-acknowledgement, you will have many opportunities throughout your day to say the magic words, "Yes, I did that!" Then you get to enjoy all the benefits mentioned in the previous paragraph.

This is so important because groundbreaking research in neuroscience and positive psychology has proven that happiness is not the result of success. Happiness is the precursor to success. Almost everyone gets this backwards and mistakenly believes that when they obtain success, then they will be happy. However, this never works.

A classic example of this is the mid-life crisis. People experiencing a mid-life crisis have obtained the material things and the successes but then realize that they are not happy or fulfilled.

Whenever we make our happiness conditional on something else (I can be happy when I am in a relationship, when I have more money in the bank, when I lose 20 pounds . . .), we deprive ourselves of the opportunity to be happy and enjoy life right now! This is living life on the layaway plan and that is simply not a good strategy.

For more on this, I recommend that you read *The Happiness Advantage* by Shawn Achor. He says, "Happiness and optimism actually fuel performance and achievement – giving us the competitive edge that I call the Happiness Advantage."

Self-acknowledgement is a great tool to create happiness and optimism.

HOW TO
SELF-ACKNOWLEDGE

The "how to" for self-acknowledgement is the same as for when you acknowledge others. State what you did or the result you produced, without opinion or judgment, with a tone of appreciation, curiosity, or surprise.

The only difference is substituting "I" for "You." "I exercised this morning!" rather than "You exercised this morning!"

You can acknowledge yourself for big things and you can also acknowledge yourself for small things. Create this habit and see what it does for you.

Try it now. Ask yourself, "What do I want to be acknowledged for?" Then acknowledge yourself.

Go ahead. Don't worry. I'll wait.

SELF-ACKNOWLEDGEMENT
ELIMINATES SUFFERING

Self-acknowledgement is also a fabulous tool for eliminating suffering.

Allow me to explain why.

People are great at beating up on themselves in their own heads when they under-perform, do not live up to their expectations, or make mistakes.

The only thing this does is create suffering. It certainly does not create positive change. Yet people keep doing it – over and over and over.

This is because people have collapsed a distinction. They are confusing their various roles in life with their identity, with who they really are.

David Sandler, founder of the Sandler Sales Institute, created this really useful distinction between identity and role. Sandler realized that successful sales training was more than just teaching techniques. In *You Can't Teach a Kid to Ride a Bike at a Seminar*, Sandler said that people also need to understand human dynamics. They need to understand "...the importance of separating 'what you R,' that is, the roles you play, from 'who you I,' your identity."

Our identity is a perfect ten! Always! Imagine holding a newborn baby. Could you imagine anything sillier than thinking, "Wow! You are messed up! You are not okay! You need to be fixed!" Of course not! You would not think any of that.

When my first daughter was born, I could not speak louder than a whisper for three days. I was so in awe and stunned by the miracle of it all. Well, that is who you are at your core, too. You are a miracle. You have vast potential. You are a perfect ten!

Then on top of this amazing miracle that is you, there are all the roles you play in life: career, parent, significant other, money maker, bill payer, person who exercises, volunteer, friend, soccer parent, and on and on.

We can perform anywhere from great to horribly in each of these different roles. Regardless of how we perform, our identity is still a perfect ten. However, we often forget that and then we suffer.

I see this all the time in my work with clients. People are beating themselves senseless because they are under-performing in a specific role and think that it is their identity. They mistakenly believe that this role performance is really who they are.

When this happens, self-worth, self-esteem, and self-confidence plummet.

Self-acknowledgement takes away the judgment and opinion. Instead, self-acknowledgement puts our focus on our role. It puts our focus on what we did rather than who we are. "I arrived late." That is just what I did. I am not good or bad because of this. When I take out the judgment, all that remains is a statement of fact. Acknowledgement keeps us focused on the facts rather than on our judgment-laden story about what happened.

"I (action verb)" is very different from "I am." Compare the feelings created by "I arrived late" with "I am an idiot, I was late." Even if we remove the overt judgment of "I am an idiot" and just use "I was late," there is still judgment there. It might be subtle, yet feel the difference between "I arrived late" and "I was late." Notice how there is a sort of sinking feeling with "I was late." It ends on a down note.

"I was late" has victim energy to it, a sort of helplessness, an implied "there is nothing I can do about this." "Am or was" equals my identity. That is who I am. I am late. My identity is lateness. Again, this is all very subtle but it is there.

"I arrived late" puts me in control. I am responsible for this result. This allows me to move forward and creates the possibility for different action next time.

Acknowledgement is about a role and about what I did, not who I am.

We will go into this in greater depth in two later chapters, *Acknowledgement As Feedback* and *Acknowledgement and Peak Performance*.

DAILY
SELF-ACKNOWLEDGEMENT

Self-acknowledgement can be one of the most powerful uses of acknowledgement especially when you can find a way to do it every day.

Every evening when I am winding down, I reflect on my day and ask myself, "What did I do today that worked and didn't work?" I write the answers down in a journal. Writing them down is important because then you get to document your self-acknowledgements. Plus, writing them down helps you to both celebrate and own the results that you produced.

It might look something like this:

Monday

What Worked	What Didn't Work
Went to CrossFit	Ate a bag of potato chips
Walked the dog	Overcooked the pasta
Cooked family dinner	Forgot to return phone call
Snuggled with my kid	Late for appointment

Continue this daily practice and you will be amazed at what you notice and the positive results it produces in your life. Try this right now. Get out a piece of paper and write down four things you did in the last 24-hours that worked and four things that did not work. They can be big or small. How does that make you feel?

Once you get good at self-acknowledgement, four a day is probably not enough, but in the beginning people often find it challenging. If that is the case with you, just find two or three to start. But, don't cheat yourself and only look at what worked, also take the time to look at what did not work. This can be difficult in the beginning, but after a little practice, acknowledging what did not work will become easier.

Over time, you will find that the practice of looking at what did not work is extremely valuable in your growth and development as a leader, a parent, a friend, and a human being.

SELF-ACKNOWLEDGEMENT AT THE POLICE ACADEMY

Years ago, I worked at the Houston Police Academy as a physical fitness and defensive tactics instructor. One of my main responsibilities was to work with the police cadets who were unable to pass the physical fitness or firearms strength test. My job was to take these cadets and provide them with specialized training. The goal was to get them up to speed so that they could pass these tests, graduate from the academy and get out on the streets.

In one of my classes, there was a woman who was making a career change. She had been a teacher and was now training to become a police officer. This woman ended up in both of my remedial training sessions. She was smart and a hard worker, but she lacked proficiency in some of the physical skills that she needed in order to graduate.

As we worked together, I noticed that she was very ambitious. One day while we were talking she revealed to me that she had the goal to graduate number one in her class. She wanted to be the top cadet. She was one of twelve women in the class that also included sixty-three men. To be the top cadet would mean she would have to score better than seventy-four other people in academics, firearms, and driving.

Since she was a former teacher, the academics were no problem. Her challenge was with the shooting and the driving. I told her I would help her to achieve her goal. I had her meet me at my office twice a week on her lunch break.

One of the techniques I taught her was self-acknowledgement.

Being as ambitious as she was, she was very hard on herself when she made mistakes. Also, she would tend to focus on the mistakes long after they had actually happened. In effect, she was reinforcing what she could not do rather than building capacity and capability.

I gave her this assignment: each time she got out of the police car after a training run or came off the shooting range, she was to write down three things she did on each trial that worked and three things she did that did not work. She did this religiously through the rest of her driving and firearms training.

As you can probably imagine, her driving scores began to improve and so did her shooting scores. She was able to focus on what was working and let go of what did not work. Instead of beating herself up and carrying that into the next trial, she was able to focus on the present moment and do her best.

In the end, her shooting and driving scores were high enough and she graduated Number One in her class, an honor that only a handful of women have ever achieved in the history of the Houston Police Department.

To this day, she believes that this would not have happened if she had not had the tool of self-acknowledgement in her toolbox.

TRY IT YOURSELF

Give self-acknowledgement a try and see what happens! You will like the results!

CHAPTER NINE

Using Acknowledgement In Team Meetings

The team meeting is a specific way to use acknowledgement. A team meeting can be used in any group, formal or informal, permanent or temporary. It can be used with business teams, leadership teams, sports teams, in families, in volunteer or for-profit organizations. You can use a team meeting anywhere you have a group of people and want to create better performance.

Do not be fooled by the name "team meeting," which might sound like a project management team at work. This kind of team meeting does not have to be a formal group or even a professional group. It can be any group of people working together for any length of time.

Team meetings bring groups together to create more teamwork, connection, and cooperation. You can use a team meeting anytime that you want to create a more cohesive and connected team.

The team meeting creates an environment where the team members:

❖ Are present
❖ Pay attention
❖ Give witness

❖ Are not in judgment or opinion
❖ Show appreciation

When team meetings are held on a regular basis, people begin to:

❖ Put their attention on what is working
❖ Focus on results
❖ Have a stronger connection with other team members

HOW TO CONDUCT
A TEAM MEETING

1) Train/teach the people how a team meeting works and what an acknowledgement is.
2) Get the team into a circle.
3) Ask the team to look around the circle at the other team members and just see what they see. You can coach them a little to "notice the vitality, notice the connection, notice how lit up people are."
4) Each person has the opportunity to say something they did that worked, some result they got, something they are proud of or just want to share. It can be business or personal, small or large. Be ready to gently correct and educate people when they slip into compliments or praise. Your coaching should sound something like, "What did you do that makes you say that?"
5) People can go in any order. Your job is to be patient and stay curious until everyone is acknowledged.

6) Have everyone use the language, "I want to be acknowledged for..." Sometimes people will say something like, "I want to acknowledge myself for..." The former allows the whole team to participate in the acknowledgement. The latter turns the rest of the team members into bystanders.

7) Everyone puts his or her attention on the person getting acknowledged.

8) After the acknowledgement has been stated, everyone claps, including the person getting acknowledged.

9) After everyone is acknowledged, have the team look around the circle at the other team members again. You can ask, "Is the team the same or different than when we started? If different, how?" or "How is the team different than when we started?"

You can also add another step between 8 and 9. In this step, team members can acknowledge each other. This is for something that another team member did or a result that they produced.

Normally, the leader of the team meeting does not get acknowledged. If one of the team members asks the leader what they want to be acknowledged for, go ahead and say something that you want to be acknowledged for.

WHAT TO PAY ATTENTION TO

In order to make your team meeting the most effective and beneficial, you need to be willing to do some coaching. Also, there are a few things you want to pay attention to.

Pay attention to the person when they say what they want to be acknowledged for. See if it really lights them up. Separate the story from the "action or results." If it does not light them up, you will want to drill down and create clarity by asking, "What did you do that you want to be acknowledged for?" Or you can say, "Ok, that is the story about it; what did you do that you want to be acknowledged for?" Ask again, "What specifically did you do?" or "What result did you get?"

Many times, especially when acknowledgement is a new concept, people ask to be acknowledged for things that are not actions or results. For example, Susan might say, "I want to be acknowledged for having a great day yesterday."

Having a great day is a nice thing but it is not something a person can get acknowledged for. In this case, ask Susan, "What did you *do* that makes you say you had a great day?" This is often a new way of thinking for people; make sure to give Susan time to think about what she did. If she says, "I don't know" that just means she needs more time to think about it. So say something like, "That is OK. Go ahead and take a minute to think about something you did yesterday that worked." And then wait.

Here is another example. Joe might say, "We got our project done on time." This is tricky because it is what happened, but acknowledging "we" is not possible. In this example, Joe is not saying what he did to contribute to getting the project done on time. Ask Joe, "What did *you* do to contribute to getting the project done on time?" Again, give Joe time to think about it. He probably has not thought about it in this way. You want to acknowledge Joe for something specific that he did.

It is important for each team member to participate both in asking for acknowledgement and in clapping for others and giving attention. If someone is not participating, you cannot let that slide. It will greatly impact what you are trying to create by having the team meeting in the first place.

It is also important for each team member to personally say what he or she wants to be acknowledged for. Resist the temptation to speak for them.

Do not ask questions to get more details about the acknowledgement. Keep in mind that we do not have to understand a word of the acknowledgement. As long as it is something they did and it lights them up, we can acknowledge them.

If it does not light them up, then you can ask clarifying questions to help them get to something that does light them up.

Ask the team to get curious about and put their attention on the person getting acknowledged. Your job is to keep the team's attention on the person being acknowledged.

Do not allow team members to ask any questions about what they said or add to the story. That can be done outside the team meeting.

If a person asks to be acknowledged for something that did not work, go ahead, yield to their request, and acknowledge it. However, typically in team meetings we do not want to encourage people to say what did not work. To create better performance, we want people's attention on what is working.

Team meetings should be light-hearted, fun and inspiring. Everyone should leave the meeting feeling better and experiencing more vitality than when they arrived.

ALMOST A TEAM MEETING

Back in the 1980s, my friend, Kate, used to work at Whole Foods. Here is her experience of Whole Foods' version of a team meeting.

> Each team at the store (grocery, produce, cashiers, etc.) held its own monthly team meeting.
>
> At the end of each meeting we would do something called "Brags and Boasts." Team members would acknowledge each other by saying things like:
>
> ❖ "Hey, I really appreciate Emily staying late for the first part of my shift when I got here late last week."
> ❖ "I think the new kid is doing great. Very fast in the Express Lane."
> ❖ "I want to thank June for always being so cheerful. Just looking at her smile cheers me up sometimes when I'm having a bad day."
> ❖ etc., etc.
>
> "Brags and Boasts" really meant a lot to people. It made us feel like more of a team and caused us to work together better and be willing to go the extra mile for each other.

We only talked about other people though. We never boasted about anything that we had done ourselves. And sometimes that hurt. If you had done some really hard extra work and no one else praised you for it, you kind of felt left out."

It seems very clear that Whole Foods was really making an effort to create a positive work environment and to build stronger teams. But Kate's comments indicate that something big was missing from these meetings.

Can you identify what was missing from these meetings?

That is right ~ there was no way for people to ask for and get acknowledged for what was important to them. They had to hope that someone else mentioned the important thing or else it would go unacknowledged. The result was that at times Kate felt disappointed and left out.

Obviously, the intention of these meetings was not to make people feel disappointed and left out. I am sure the intention was the opposite, to build team and community and to create a positive work environment. It just did not always work because people could not ask for the acknowledgement they craved.

Do you think that after a meeting where she did not get recognized for what was important to her, Kate was more or less motivated at work?

RESULTS FROM A REAL
TEAM MEETING

Recently, I taught a young leader how to conduct a team meeting. Soon afterwards, he told me a story about how he used a team meeting to improve a team's effectiveness.

He was working on a volunteer project outside of work. One day, just out of curiosity, he led a "team meeting" before they began their project for that day. No one in the group knew about the tool of acknowledgement and he was a virtual beginner.

He admitted that he was a bit surprised to see there was more cooperation in the group than he had ever noticed before. The group was also more effective and everyone seemed to have more fun.

The point here is not to wait until you think you get it or are good at it. Find a group of people and give it a go. Start doing team meetings now and learn on the job.

GUIDELINES ON WHEN, WHERE, AND HOW
OFTEN TO HAVE TEAM MEETINGS

Have team meetings any time you want to create cohesion, connection, and attention in a group of people.

The "team" in the team meeting is the people who are participating in that particular meeting. In other words, this may not be a formal or permanent team. In fact, this exact group may never come together again. But for this particular moment in time, they are your team.

In most environments, I do not think it is possible to have too many team meetings. Most of the time, we do not have enough team meetings.

In general, people are starved for acknowledgement and conversation based on real results, which is exactly what a team meeting provides.

I have seen leaders create high-performance environments with a group of strangers in a very short time by having a team meeting every five minutes. This creates intensity, results, and excitement in the group that I have rarely seen anywhere else in my career. Getting acknowledged moves people to higher states of attention, awareness, and performance like no other tool or technique I have ever seen.

Am I suggesting you should have team meetings every five minutes? Probably not, but you should have them more often than you think you should.

Some examples of great times and places to have team meetings are:

- Before a project meeting
- After a project meeting
- Before an employee's annual evaluation
- Before a volunteer board meeting
- Before the beginning of the workday
- At the end of the workday
- During family dinner
- Before a sporting event
- After a sporting event
- Before a sports team practice
- After a sports team practice

You should be starting to get the idea that you can have a team meeting any time and anywhere a group of people assembles to get something done. You can have a team meeting at the beginning, in the middle of, or at the end of any meeting, project, event, or game.

Another good time to have a team meeting is when things are starting to get off track or go awry. The team meeting will often have the effect of refocusing the team and lead to better performance.

When you have a team meeting, eliminate as many distractions as possible. Stay calm. Do not rush the meeting. Give people time to consider what they want to be acknowledged for. Keep your attention and the group's attention on the person being acknowledged. And most importantly, HAVE FUN!

I firmly believe that any authentic and integrity-based attempt at acknowledgement, even from a total beginner, is better and far more impactful than most of the other things people do to try to contribute to others.

Don't be afraid to give team meetings a try. And after you do give it a try, find someone to acknowledge you for leading a team meeting!

CHAPTER TEN

Acknowledgement In Leadership

Leadership. Now that is a hot topic. What does acknowledgement have to do with leadership? Acknowledgement has everything to do with leadership!

THE FIRST DISTINCTION IN LEADERSHIP ~ LEADERSHIP IS NOT MANAGEMENT

In order to effectively explore leadership, we need an understanding of the distinction between management and leadership. Management and leadership are often thought of as the same thing. We use these words interchangeably or, worse yet, collapse them into the same thing. In reality, they are two very different things.

Management was invented to manage things, processes, and paper. Management was never intended to be applied to people. People are not things. When we try to manage people, they resist. Think about it ~ do you really like to be managed? Of course not! Being managed is uncomfortable and not enjoyable.

The verb *manage* comes from the Italian *maneggiare* (to handle - especially tools), which, in turn, derives from the Latin *manus* (hand). Really, who wants to be handled?

Wikipedia defines management as, "Organization and coordination of the activities of an enterprise in accordance with certain policies and in achievement of clearly defined objectives."

Management is often included as a factor of production, along with machines, materials, and money.

Daniel Pink, in his book, *Drive*, talks about the problem with managing people.

> We forget sometimes that 'management' does not emanate from nature. It's not like a tree or a river. It's like a television or a bicycle. It's something that humans invented. As the strategy guru Gary Hamel has observed, management is a technology, and, it's a technology that has grown creaky. Core management hasn't changed much in a hundred years. Its central ethic remains control; its chief tools remain extrinsic motivators. That leaves it largely out of sync with the nonroutine, right-brain abilities on which many of the world's economies now depend. But could its most glaring weakness run deeper?
>
> Is management, as it's currently constituted, out of sync with human nature itself?
>
> The idea of management (that is, management of people rather than management of, say, supply chains) is built on certain assumptions about the basic natures of those being managed. It presumes that to take action or move forward, we need a

prod - that absent a reward or punishment, we'd remain happily and inertly in place. It also presumes that once people do get moving, they need direction that without a firm and reliable guide, they'd wander.

But is that really our fundamental nature? Or, to use yet another computer metaphor, *is* that our 'default setting'? When we enter the world are we wired to be passive and inert? Or are we wired to be active and engaged.

I'm convinced it's the latter - that our basic nature is to be curious and self-directed. And I say that not because I'm a dewy-eyed idealist, but because I've been around young children and because my wife and I have three kids of our own. Have you ever seen a six-month-old or a one-year-old who's *not* curious and self-directed? I haven't. That's how we are out of the box. If, at age fourteen or forty-three, we're passive and inert, that's not because it's our nature. It's because something flipped our default setting.

That something could well be management - not merely how bosses treat us at work, but also how the broader ethos has leeched into schools, families, and many other aspects of our lives.

Perhaps management isn't *responding* to our supposedly natural state of passive inertia. Perhaps management is one of the forces that's switching our default setting and *producing* that state.

In a nutshell: Management is producing under-performance by trying to create improved performance. This happens in business far more often than any of us should be okay with!

Management is a technology from the 1850s. It is old and it is not working very well anymore. This begs the question, has it ever worked?

As a society, we believe that when you reward behavior, you get more of it, and when you punish behavior; you get less of that behavior. However, this is seldom the case.

Daniel Pink scrutinized this idea. He looked at fifty years of research in social science and found out that this is not true all of the time, or even as much as we think.

For any task that requires more than a rudimentary skill level, rewards consistently decrease performance. If/then motivators (e. g., "if you do this then you will receive this") are effective for mechanical or routine tasks that have a set of rules to follow. Once you ask a person to do work, which requires judgment or is creative, complicated, or complex, if/then motivators do not work anymore. In other words, if/then motivators are effective in job situations where people are not required to think, where robots can replace people. In all other situations, if/then motivators decrease performance.

Pink also said that punishment does not work. Human beings are complicated. Calibrating better rewards and punishment is not the answer.

Effective motivation is subtle, and most current motivation techniques and strategies are anything but subtle. If you want to effectively motivate for high-level work, you have to move on to something new. We have that "something new." That something new is acknowledgement!

To really help people at work, we have to stop trying to control people, stop trying to motivate them with money, stuff or even punishment, and start acknowledging them for what they accomplish.

Teresa M. Amabile and Steven J. Kramer conducted a groundbreaking, multiyear study where they tracked hundreds of knowledge workers. On a day-to-day basis, they tracked daily activities, emotions, and motivation levels.

Amabile and Kramer said, "We now know what the top motivator of performance is . . . It's progress. On days when workers have the sense they're making headway in their jobs, or when they receive support that helps them overcome obstacles, their emotions are most positive and their drive to succeed is at its peak. On days when they feel they are spinning their wheels or encountering roadblocks to meaningful accomplishment, their moods and motivation are lowest."

Daniel Pink's work and Amabile and Kramer's study show why the tool of acknowledgement is so desperately needed in the workplace.

Amabile and Kramer reported the two factors that create the most positive emotions in employees are making significant progress and receiving support. Acknowledgement excels at doing both of those things. Acknowledgement allows the employees to take a clear look at their accomplishments, to recognize the people who supported them, and to receive support.

That sounds very different from what is happening on a daily basis in most companies.

People are being chastised or even punished for mistakes. They are being subjected to managers and evaluation systems that encourage competition among team members. Work environments are generally focused on what is not working. Is it any wonder that people are not happy and inspired at work?

Daniel Pink's research did find that money matters, but not as much as we think it does. People need to be paid fairly and paid enough in order to get to their intrinsic motivation. If they are not being paid fairly or enough, they will get stuck on this issue. Once you pay people enough to get the issue of money off the table, they are free to access their intrinsic motivation.

There is a huge myth out there that people will do better if they are effectively managed. They do not perform better! They just feel managed and processed.

Leadership on the other hand, when done well, is really respectful and graceful and produces remarkable results. Think about the great leaders you have had, or know of. Have you ever had a leader that you would run through a brick wall for? Chances are you are not the only one that felt that way. Most, if not all, team members probably felt the same way. What was he or she doing that made you feel that way?

Great leadership is a funny thing. We know it when we see it, but it is almost impossible to describe. What are these great leaders doing? What exactly is the essence of a great leader?

I searched Amazon.com for "leadership books." There were 71,461 results. Obviously, we are doing a lot of thinking and writing about leadership. Yet we are still experiencing a leadership crisis in America. From small mom-and-pop shops to large, multi-national corporations, great leadership is still a great mystery.

The dictionary does not help. All of the definitions of leadership have the word leader in them. All of the definitions of leader contain the word lead. Finally, the word lead used as a verb has at least thirty-four definitions. So, leadership is done by leaders who lead in at least one of thirty-four different ways. Well, that clears things up.

No wonder we have a leadership crisis! How can anyone be clear about what leadership is, much less know how to actually do it?

THE SECOND DISTINCTION IN LEADERSHIP ~ LEADERS CREATE RECEPTIVITY

The best definition of leadership I have ever heard was from Martin Sage, Transpersonal Coach and founder of Sage University. He said that true leadership is, "creating enough curiosity so that people will follow you, just to see what happens next."

True leadership is not pushing, but pulling. True leadership is about not forcing people through their resistance, but creating receptivity. Think of the best leader you know. This is probably what they do. People want to follow them.

This is the second distinction in leadership. A great leader does not push people through their resistance. Rather, a great leader creates receptivity. And guess what? Acknowledgement creates receptivity - receptivity within people and also receptivity in the environments in which we work, live, and play.

On the other hand, management, punishment, and even motivation techniques create resistance.

Resistance is the opposition from one thing to another or from one person or group to another. Resistance is synonymous with obstinacy and defiance.

Creating opposition, obstinacy and defiance is the antithesis of great leadership and is certainly not effective, productive, or enjoyable ~ for all parties involved.

When people receive enough acknowledgement, their resistance goes away, dissatisfaction and frustration end, and whining and complaining stop. They simply have no use for those things any more.

The reason unsuccessful leaders struggle with leadership is that these people are unwittingly trying to manage instead of lead. Who can blame them?

Management looks and seems easier. If people were more like machines, the leader's job would be easier because they could just manage. (Un)fortunately people are not machines. People have dreams, desires, and needs. And among their most powerful needs is the need to be productive and useful and contribute to something.

When people get acknowledged, it becomes clear to them that they are productive and they can see how they are making a contribution. I know what you are thinking; they should know these things without having to be acknowledged for them. It might seem that way, but that is not how people really are.

The simplest and best way for you to improve your leadership is to find a way to create more receptivity in your people and your team. To do that, you need to put your ego and your management training aside and acknowledge people. Acknowledge them a lot!

ACKNOWLEDGEMENT ALLOWS
FOR LEARNING

Acknowledgement allows people to learn ~ to really learn from both their successes and their mistakes. When we take the judgment out of performance, people can objectively look at what worked and what did not work, and learn from both.

Most people are so busy suffering from the judgment they put on themselves or that we put on them for making mistakes that they cannot truly learn from their mistakes.

Also, if people are being judged for what does not work, they are likely spending a lot of time and energy covering up or hiding their mistakes. Obviously, this does not contribute to productivity, a positive work environment or employee satisfaction.

Have you ever learned about a mistake an employee made long after the fact? Often, it is long enough afterwards that a small mistake, one that could have been easily fixed or rectified, grew into a big deal with big consequences. Now, as the leader, you have to deal with these unnecessary consequences.

I call this "hiding a campfire, until it becomes a bonfire" and it happens all the time. Why did that employee fail to tell you about his or her small or big mistake? Could it be because he knew there would be a lot of judgment and make wrong from you if he told you?

The pain of the immediate judgment and make wrong seems like too much so they take a chance and attempt to hide it from you. Consequently, little things that you could easily fix or handle in the moment do not get reported ~ only to be noticed when it has grown out of proportion. The bad news is that the responsibility for this lies at your feet. As the leader, you have created that environment.

What if you had a system of acknowledgement in place, a system with no judgment? Could you change the whole culture of your organization? I believe you can. I have seen it happen! At a minimum, you can certainly increase productivity and performance of your team.

Just eliminating people's fear of punishment would automatically increase communication, productivity, receptivity, and connection. It would also raise levels of creativity and performance.

RESISTANCE AND RECEPTIVITY

I have been working with and observing people in environments of leadership and achievement for years. Over that time, I have observed that all performance can be boiled down to one simple distinction. As a leader, you encounter this distinction every day. Until now, you have been ill-equipped to deal with it effectively.

This simple distinction is resistance versus receptivity. I believe this is the most important distinction in human performance. This is a key variable in human performance. People can either be in resistance or in receptivity. If people are resistant, performance decreases.

If they are receptive, performance increases. It really is that simple.

The mistake most leaders make is spending a lot of time and energy trying to push people through their resistance instead of creating receptivity. Pushing people generally only creates more resistance. The trouble is that this is the only tool or strategy most leaders, managers, and parents have. Until now!

Unquestionably, acknowledgement creates receptivity. As we have already covered, praise, appreciation, and compliments all create resistance.

TRADITIONAL FEEDBACK
CREATES RESISTANCE

What about traditional feedback? What does that create?

Feedback also creates resistance. I hate to burst your bubble, but people do not learn from your "feedback." They endure or ignore it but they do not learn or improve from it.

Tony Schwartz, CEO of The Energy Project, said, "Ultimately, we'd be better off eliminating concepts like 'feedback' and 'constructive criticism' from our lexicons altogether. They're polarizing, and mostly destructive."

Have you ever asked someone, "Can I give you some feedback?" Do they jump up and down, happy and receptive, hollering at the top of their lungs "Yes, yes, yes"? Or is there hesitation, followed by a meek "Yes," or an "I guess?" Guess what? They are now in resistance.

If you watch their vitality, you will see it go down. If you watch their curiosity, you will see it go into full retreat. People are conditioned to brace themselves for feedback. Why? Feedback is judgment and as I have said over and over, people hate to be judged. Judgment is painful!

People will say "Yes" to feedback because they feel like they do not have any choice, especially if you are their boss. But they do not really want it. They automatically become resistant even before you begin to deliver the feedback.

For this, we can thank the thousands of management consultants who have been paid millions of dollars to teach managers the feedback sandwich. You may have even been taught this technique. It goes something like this: When you have some corrective or negative feedback to give someone, sandwich it in between two positive pieces of feedback.

This does not work with people. People are amazingly savvy and perceptive. Once a manger has done this to them more than a couple of times, they catch on. The biggest problem with the feedback sandwich is that all three statements are judgmental. Even with the positive comments, the receiver still has to wade through the judgment to "hear" the positive, and this is amazingly difficult to do. Then they brace for impact. In the end, they do not hear anything and have a difficult time making any improvement.

Have you ever wondered why people don't improve after you have given them feedback? Now you know why. Feedback does not work to improve people or their performance. Acknowledgement does.

This might at least partially explain why 65% of Americans in the workplace reported they received no positive feedback in the previous twelve months (Tom

Rath and Gallup Organizations). Maybe they were fed a steady stream of feedback sandwiches. That is enough to give anyone a bad feeling in their gut!

DISCOVERING WHAT IS IMPORTANT

Recently, I taught a group of leaders from a construction company how to conduct a team meeting. This was part of their leadership training. These leaders already had the tool of acknowledgement but I had not taught them how to have a team meeting. After a ninety-minute training session on how to conduct a team meeting, they were sent back to work with the assignment to conduct three or four of their own team meetings over the next thirty days.

The following month, I asked them what happened when they conducted their team meetings. What worked? What did not work? What did they learn?

Some of their answers were pretty predictable. Their employees were initially resistant to the idea, but after just a couple of meetings, they started to come around. Once people started embracing the team meeting, the leaders reported a very inspiring thing. When they listened, really listened to what their people asked to be acknowledged for, they began to learn things about their people they did not know. Most importantly, they could hear what was most important to their people. A few reported that they learned more about their employees in the team meetings than they ever had before. (This was a well-established, family-owned business with many long-term employees.)

Typically, leaders assume they know what is important to the employees. When a leader understands what is really important to the employees and what achievements and results are meaningful to them, the leader can then begin to help the employees do more of those things. The leaders now have the necessary information to put the employees into positions that allow for success and for results that are the most meaningful to the employees. This is effective and powerful leadership!

True leadership is knowing what is important to your people and then putting them into situations that allow them to do or achieve what is most important to them.

Remember, true leadership is not pushing, but pulling. True leadership is about not forcing people through their resistance, but creating receptivity.

You can greatly improve your leadership simply by adopting the tool of acknowledgement because it does such a great job of producing receptivity.

Leaders are doing the best they can with the tools they have. The tool of acknowledgement is an unparalleled opportunity to upgrade your leadership. People are suffering immensely in the workplace and a lot of that has to do with their leaders.

Evelyn, one of our content editors who works at a financial services firm, was so moved by this chapter that she left us this note.

"I can't agree enough. I don't think it can be driven home deeply enough how painful this whole feed-back/judgment thing is ~ even at the subtle, yet mature level most of us tend to hold our working personas. And don't we tend to avoid pain like the plague unless we're masochists?"

118

As a leader, do you want people avoiding the pain of your judgment, or do you want them enjoying the freedom and fulfillment of your acknowledgement?

It is your choice!

CHAPTER ELEVEN

Acknowledgement In Sports

Acknowledgement in sports is an interesting application. Nowhere else do we give more "Good jobs!" and "Atta-boys!" than on the playing field. Athletes recognize each other in a lot of ways: pointing, verbalizing, patting each other on the rear end, and high fives, just to name a few. These are all great ways of recognizing each other and appreciating the effort the other person just made.

ACKNOWLEDGEMENT BETWEEN ATHLETES

In an athlete-to-athlete relationship, these methods work pretty well. Because of the immediacy of the praise, the other person is able to own the result they just produced or the action they took. So in this case the praise points in the direction of a repeatable action. The praise is almost like a request to do that again. "Hit the ball like that again," etc. The athlete just did something positive and that is what is being pointed out. The athlete then gets to have that moment of self-discovery where they think, "Yes, I did do that!"

But what about when an athlete messes up? What happens when they miss a pass, drop a routine fly ball, blow a defensive assignment, or miss a basket?

Interestingly enough, athletes have evolved a way of saying "I messed up" in a way that allows them to get acknowledged for their error. When someone makes a mistake, have you ever heard him or her say "My bad"? This phrase has made its way into mainstream culture.

This is a way of acknowledging and asking to be acknowledged for messing up. In saying, "My bad," you own the result you produced.

I believe this strategy evolved out of sports where an athlete needs to move on from a mistake very quickly in order to minimize the impact of that mistake on the next play. Acknowledging the mistake does exactly this.

Not only that, but it also allows the athlete's teammates to let go and move on as well. I love it when a teammate of mine acknowledges himself or herself with a "my bad." This makes it really easy for me to let go of my emotions of frustration or disappointment and get my head back in the game.

The idea of "my bad" is actually a great strategy for letting go and moving on. This can be used all over your life: sports, business, relationships, parenting, leadership and . . . Acknowledge what you did that did not work and then move on!

When was the last time you messed up? (Are we measuring in minutes or hours?) It happens to everyone. How much time, energy, and attention did you put on the mistake? If you are like most people, the answer is A LOT! Have you ever held on to your mistake to the extent that it impacted your next action or, worse yet, kept you from taking the next action?

The problem is that if your attention is on the mistake, it cannot be on the next golf shot, pitch, or project. Attention can only be in one place at a time. Acknowledging the mistake, or what you did that did not work, allows you to move on quickly from the mistake. This is exactly what athletes are trying to accomplish when they say "My bad." "Yep. I messed up. I want to be acknowledged and I am moving on."

What if we all had the ability to move on from mistakes quickly? Well, now you do.

ACKNOWLEDGEMENT AT THE CROSSFIT WORLD CHAMPIONSHIP

In 2011, I worked with an elite team of CrossFit athletes – three men and three women competing together as a team. They were training for the 2011 CrossFit Games, which is the world championship for CrossFit.

One of the tools I taught them to use in their training and competition was the tool of acknowledgement. Before they received the tool of acknowledgement, they had trouble communicating with one another as a team, especially in terms of correcting errors or talking about what did not work. I taught them how to have a team meeting and how to ask for acknowledgement from their team, both for what worked and what did not work.

They practiced this for a few weeks leading up to the competition and carried it into the three-day competition. Here is what team member Lt. Susie Tannery, SC, a lieutenant in the US Naval Reserves and a mom of two, said about acknowledgement.

Acknowledgement really helped me during my team training for the CrossFit Games 2011. Ever feeling like I might be the weakest link on the Bayou City CrossFit Team, the team meetings and acknowledgement allowed me to acknowledge my strengths and abilities and overcome my insecurities.

I was really happy with my mental performance at the CrossFit Games. Acknowledgement training prior to the event really helped me to tune out any negativity and concentrate on what I could and did do well. In retrospect, I could also see what I failed on. This allowed me to relish in what I did well and to concentrate on what I would need to improve upon.

Acknowledgement really opens up communication, within yourself and especially in a team setting. Essentially, you are able to clear the air with your team, move on to the next and most important task and not dwell on anything that did not go as planned.

What a great tool. I feel it has made me grow as a person and I continue to use acknowledgement in my day-to-day tasks, with clients (Susie is also a CrossFit coach) and in my own training.

Katie Russell is another CrossFit coach who was also a member of the 2011 team. She came back from the games a believer in acknowledgement as a tool to help her athletes. She implemented acknowledgement into her ladies' strength program. After each of their training sessions, she would have a team meeting and simply ask them to say something they had done in the past few days that they were proud of. It could be anything. It did not have to be something they had done in their training.

They followed the team meeting guidelines. Each person asked to be acknowledged for something they did and got acknowledged by the others in the group.

To everyone's surprise (except mine), some amazing things happened.

Near the end of the program, I asked the group, "What is different since you have been getting acknowledged in the team meetings?" The stories were amazing and shocking even to me.

Katie is a young CrossFit coach, who had only one hour of training on the tool of acknowledgement and a few weeks of experience with the tool. She then implemented it in her training program and produced amazing results.

Here is an example of these unexpected results. This comes from one of Katie's students, Serena, a life-long athlete and a Corporate Banking Representative.

> Ever since I can remember, people have always said I couldn't do this or that because I was too small or too petite, or that I didn't have the right build. I tried to always use this as fuel to prove everyone wrong. However after hearing that all my life, I believed it to a certain degree.
>
> I joined Katie's 'Babes and Barbells' lifting program. The program helped me to get stronger, but unexpectedly and even

better, it helped me gain confidence and acceptance of myself. Katie required us to say something we wanted to be acknowledged for after every workout. This made me realize I was progressing in more areas than I realized. Most of all, it made me think of myself in a positive way. Every week I began to feel better and better about myself. I wasn't ashamed to look at myself in the mirror anymore, I didn't criticize myself like I did before, I came to like what I saw and who I saw. I was able to use the positive thinking in more than just CrossFit, and ultimately this practice has brought me to a better place within myself.

Wouldn't you like to get that kind of return on investment in the stock market? Just a few minutes a week spent on acknowledgement completely changed Serena's life. That is the amazing, potential power of acknowledgement!

ACKNOWLEDGEMENT BETWEEN COACHES AND ATHLETES

The coach and athlete relationship is another interesting place to apply the tool of acknowledgement in sports. It is an easy way to get coach and athlete on the same page.

Katie tells another story about Val, an athlete she worked with for a couple of years. Val was a big challenge for Katie. Katie perceived Val as negative, unmotivated, and as someone who would easily get down on herself. Katie really did not know how to handle this and became increasingly frustrated with Val and with herself.

Then Val joined Katie's strength class and participated in the team meetings that Katie held after each training session. After a few weeks, something interesting happened. Val started to be more positive, motivated, and more confident.

By getting acknowledged, Val was able to focus on what was working and see it in a way that allowed her to think differently about herself.

By listening to what Val wanted to be acknowledged for, Katie was able to hear what was really important to Val. Katie began to understand Val better as an athlete and a human being. This caused both the athlete and the coach to relax and to be able to grow their trust and their connection.

Both athlete and coach said that acknowledgement completely transformed their relationship.

Here is what Katie said about the tool of acknowledgement.

> Acknowledgement has changed our (Katie and Val) relationship so much. Before when she would give up on herself in class, I would roll my eyes and ignore her because I figured it was the same old excuses I had heard before. She is overtraining, not eating right, drank too much. . .
>
> After she joined the strength program I found out that Val really just needed to be

around other women who also experienced 'off' days. Val thought she had to be on her 'A' game every day and consequently when she came across a weakness, she would give up.

We did acknowledgements in my strength program. This helped her focus more on her strengths and be happy with the things she is good at. She quickly realized how much stuff she excels at and her weaknesses were not so much of a big deal anymore. Now in class if there is something she struggles with, she reminds herself to stay positive and work through it.

Every woman in Katie's strength class indicated that in some way acknowledgement had an immensely positive impact on them. Many of them talked about the value outside of their fitness practice. They reported that having a place to get acknowledged really spurred them on to do better and try harder, not only on their fitness endeavors, but also at work and even as a parent. They also found it really valuable to have a place to talk about their accomplishments without it sounding like they were bragging.

An amazing and unintended happy consequence for Katie is that just by using the tools with her athletes, she became a better coach.

When asked how acknowledgement has impacted her as a coach, Katie said:

Acknowledgement has impacted me in a big way. I finally realized that different people need different treatment and that many people need different treatment on a day-to-day basis. Some people need to be acknowledged, some need to be babied, some want to be left alone, and some want to be yelled at. Whatever coaching they need from me, it's my job to figure that out and not get frustrated. I have learned that most of the time what is going on with them has very little to do with me and everything to with them.

There is a great opportunity for all sports coaches to use acknowledgement to transform their relationships with their athletes, as well as to transform the athletes themselves. Katie, Serena, Val, and Susie were all transformed as athletes and human beings from having embraced and experienced the power of acknowledgement.

Coaches tend to do a lot of praising and that is okay. However, I challenge you as a coach to replace some of that praise and recognition with acknowledgement. When you do, watch what happens.

I am 100% certain acknowledgement makes athletes perform better. In addition to creating better athletes, acknowledgement also creates better teammates, better students, better citizens, and, ultimately, better people. Isn't that what all coaches who have a clue are trying to accomplish ~ win games while creating better human beings?

Coaches, here is your opportunity. Go for it!

CHAPTER TWELVE

Acknowledgement In Parenting

Acknowledgement can make parenting a total joy. Yes, I know that is a bold statement. I can confidently say this because I have experienced this first-hand. As a parent, I do not know how I would cope without the tool of acknowledgement.

In my own parenting, I do not compliment or appreciate. I acknowledge. Occasionally, I will use praise after an acknowledgement. "You finished your homework!" Pause! "You are a rock star!"

Rather than getting caught in the common parenting traps of arguments, conflict and emotionally-charged judgments and opinions - all of which create resistance and resentment – acknowledgement allows you to have clean, simple, and highly effective communication with your child.

Acknowledgement takes you out of the parenting style of parent as police officer, guardian of what is right, or mommy-and-daddy-know-best and turns both your attention and your children's attention towards progress and success. You end up on the same team pulling towards the same goals.

Acknowledgement can put an end to all of the games and tests that kids use, like resistance, resentment, sullenness, shyness, attitude, mood, and tantrums. These are things your child does to control you.

The main reason children behave this way is to get attention. They have already asked for your attention in productive ways over and over, but never got it. If they do not feel seen or heard when they act appropriately, they will eventually act out in inappropriate ways in an attempt to get attention. Negative attention is better than no attention.

Acknowledgement allows you to fix this trap, or even better, to avoid it altogether by paying close attention and actually acknowledging them.

DEALING WITH A MOOD

Imagine that your child is having a mood. If you can say, "You are having a mood" without any judgment or opinion, that feedback will bring them face-to-face with themselves where they can see that they are indeed having a mood. Chances are very good that the mood will not last much longer.

In Chapter 6, *How To Acknowledge*, I said you cannot acknowledge something that is in process or not yet completed. For the acknowledgement to really land and make an impact it has to be for a completed action.

So, "You are having a mood" is not an acknowledgement, but it is feedback. And this feedback sets the stage for further acknowledgement that will allow you to support your child to get out of his or her mood.

When your child gets out of his or her mood, life gets better for everyone!

This next story illustrates how this works.

NATE'S MOOD

Recently, my friend Lynne picked her son up at school. He was having a mood. He was frustrated and flustered by some events at school. He lost his favorite water bottle, ran out of paper and . . . he just had a bad day.

Lynne said to him, "You are having a mood." Just that one simple comment, said without a tone of judgment or opinion, allowed him to see that he was indeed having a mood.

As soon as he could see his mood, Lynne asked him what he wanted to be acknowledged for.

> Nate: I lost my favorite water bottle.
> Lynne: You lost your water bottle.
> Nate: I ran out of paper and could not finish my project.
> Lynne: You ran out of paper.

These few simple acknowledgements allowed him to shift and Lynne was able to watch the anger and confusion just drain away. In just a couple of minutes, Nate was back to being himself ~ a happy ten year old boy.

This whole process was very easy and did not meet with any resistance because acknowledgement has long been a part of their family system.

Also, Nate got to feel heard and validated because Lynne asked him what he wanted to be acknowledged for. Nate got to say what was important to him!

So often, well meaning parents will try to do something similar but instead of asking the child, the parent will think for the child and make up stories. The parent might say something like, "Looks like you had a hard day at school. Was someone mean to you?" Or, "Did you get a bad grade on your test?"

When this happens, it is now about what the parent thinks is important rather than the child. Consequently the child does not feel heard or validated.

PAYING ATTENTION ~ DEMONSTRATED

When you acknowledge what your child has done, it demonstrates to him or her that you are paying attention. This creates a tremendous sense of reassurance. Attention and reassurance are what kids want most from their parents.

LEARN, CHANGE, AND ADJUST

Almost everything that a typical parent says to his or her kids is actually all about the parent and is full of the parent's judgments and opinions. That is because parents praise, appreciate, compliment, criticize, and give feedback. When parents do this, children cannot learn from the communication or make adjustments.

Acknowledgement shows your children what they have done that works and does not work. This allows them to learn and to make adjustments. They get to create a clear vision of what they can do more of if they want to achieve positive results. They become empowered and positive behavior is reinforced.

My client Sarah, the Image and TV Expert, shares:

> My husband and I got to meet our young cousins on a weekend with extended family. The cousins (age ten and twelve) were shy, withdrawn and unengaged. My husband and I decided to implement a full court press of acknowledgement on the kids.
>
> Just 24 hours later, the kids were unrecognizable. The acknowledgement transformed them into boisterous, playful, engaged kids. They completely shifted their attitude and behavior. They became full of vitality and eager to participate in any activity. We could hardly believe that they were the same people!

Shyness is usually just one of the many games or tests that kids use.

Acknowledgement invites people, of all ages, out of these non-productive games and into something that is both more productive and more enjoyable.

ACKNOWLEDGEMENT WORKS WITH OLDER KIDS TOO

Susan, a holistic wellness practitioner from New Jersey, learned about acknowledgement in one of my classes. Susan shares:

Right after our class, I used acknowledgement with my 22-year-old son. I saw
him do something that he was not supposed
to do - smoke cigarettes on the patio.

Instead of my usual I told you not
to....blah blah blah, I calmly said, 'You
smoked outside.' Wow. He hung his head
low and said, 'I know and I am so sorry.' He
was really quite contrite.

This was a whole new type of
conversation between us. I did not raise my
voice. We did not have an unhealthy
conversation that produced no results like
we would have in the past.

He understood my disappointment and
apologized. I continue to use acknowledgement whenever he crosses a boundary
and not only does he get it, but I stay on
topic with him and I do not veer off into
stuff he did in the past. He seems to feel
much more secure with this type of
communication.

Susan concludes acknowledgement is absolutely
phenomenal for both parents and children. She highly
recommends this as a tool for great parenting. She says,
"The parent feels heard and the child feels respected
because you are simply acknowledging what actually
happened."

My friend Mary is a devoted parent as well as the
manager of a medium-sized law firm. Immediately after
she learned acknowledgment, she applied it to her
parenting.

I began to watch how I acknowledged my daughters on their schoolwork.

Last week my oldest daughter, Kelsey, came home and said that she had aced her chemistry test. Before I would have said – 'great job – you are so smart!' This time I acknowledged the effort she had put into creating flash cards to help her study. Her face lit up! I could tell it meant more to her than just me telling her she was smart.

I am becoming more aware of what happens when I give a compliment or praise and am trying to turn it into an acknowledgement of effort instead.

Acknowledgement tells your children you are here for them, you believe in them and you are in their corner. What more would you want to communicate to your child?

TEAM MEETINGS WITH YOUR CHILDREN

Do you want to really upgrade your parenting? Use team meetings with your kids. The kids will catch on really fast. In the beginning, have team meetings and just acknowledge what works. Let the kids find things to get acknowledged for and to acknowledge their siblings and parents for. You might be in for some surprises about what really matters to these people that you think you know so well.

When you have a family team meeting, everyone must be on equal footing. So, do not wear your parenting hat to the meeting; wear your teammate hat. After a few team meetings, your eight-year-old will be able to lead the meeting. I suggest that you let your kids lead some of the meetings.

A friend of mine decided to give this a try. Both he and his wife noticed how positively this impacted their daughter. "The daughter was beaming throughout the entire meeting and clearly enjoyed being in charge."

The wife also contrasted this to her childhood. Her family had family meetings. They would even vote on things. But, each parent got one vote and each of the four kids got a quarter of a vote. Consequently, the kids usually got outvoted, two to one.

She felt that the whole thing was a farce and that her opinion did not really matter.

The mother was very excited after the first family team meeting because it was everything that the family meetings of her childhood were not.

A TEN-YEAR OLD'S PERSPECTIVE

My ten-year old son has been raised his entire life with the tool of acknowledgement. From the moment he was born, we acknowledged him and we began having team meetings within his first year. Recently, I asked him how his parents' having the tool of acknowledgement has impacted him.

Here is what he said. This is a direct quote. I did not edit or change any of his words.

For me, acknowledgement is basically all I have known. Wherever I look and I see non-acknowledgement it isn't good. It makes people not get what they want because they don't ask for what they want so they get mad. When I acknowledge and get acknowledged it makes me happy and also when people get acknowledged they get happy. It is always nice to make someone happy.

If everybody acknowledged, pretty much all the world's problems would suddenly vanish. That is why acknowledgement is so important.

Having acknowledgement has made my parents exponentially (yes, he said that) better, compared to other parents who don't have acknowledgement. When parents don't have the tool, nobody gets what they want and everyone is always whining and complaining.

Hang on for a minute while I pause for a proud parent moment!

If you have whining and complaining in your family, it is time for some acknowledgement. If your kids are disinterested, uncommunicative, and there is a lack of connection, it is time for some acknowledgement. If you want to build a stronger family and create a positive, supportive, and inspired home environment, it is time for acknowledgement!

A RADICAL NEW IDEA

Consider the idea that a consistent practice of acknowledgement might be one of the best ways (if not the best) to demonstrate your love for your children.

As we covered in chapter 4, praise, appreciation, and compliments usually do not serve your children and often actually cause negative consequences, like decreased performance, decreased creativity, risk aversion, and lack of initiative.

Eventually, all of this can cause kids to stop thinking for themselves. They lose their ability to use critical thinking.

Acknowledgement equips them for the real world. They develop a results focus and can see both the positive and the negative consequences of their actions. This focus supports them to develop resiliency and persistence, qualities that are essential for success.

As a parent, what do you want? Do you really want to create resistant, fearful, and low-performing kids or do you want to create high-functioning, happy, and resilient kids?

CHAPTER THIRTEEN

Acknowledgement In Relationships

Have you noticed how often in intimate relationships people whine and complain about their significant other? Does anyone really think this is an effective relationship-strengthening strategy? Is this going to somehow make things better?

Usually, this complaining is about something the partner does repeatedly or something the partner does not do enough of.

And oftentimes, we have done our darndest to get the other person to change. We have talked to them, yelled at them, criticized them, begged them, given them the silent treatment, threatened them and . . .

The one constant in all of these activities is that we are judging them and making them wrong. This negativity coming from us automatically puts them into a state of resistance, which tremendously decreases the likelihood of positive change.

Not surprisingly, judgment is not a relationship-enhancing strategy. Being judged does not put your partner in a romantic mood.

The one thing we most likely have not tried is acknowledgement. What a novel idea ~ reinforce the positive behavior and pour your belief into your partner.

139

Try it and see what happens in your relationship. Chances are your relationship will bloom when the other person starts to feel you believe in him or her. Your partner will almost automatically believe in him or herself more.

Every time you acknowledge your partner, you are saying to them, "I really see you! I am paying attention and I believe in your ability and capacity."

Even acknowledging seemingly small things creates this effect in your partner. "You took out the trash." "You called me just to say 'Hi'." "You went grocery shopping." Although seemingly trivial, these acknowledgements send a strong, positive message.

My client Sarah, the Image and TV Expert, says:

> Acknowledgement may have saved my marriage. Before I had the tool of acknowledgement, I verbally beat the heck out of my husband, complaining about everything he did wrong and nagging him to change. I don't think our marriage could have survived my constant nagging and complaining.
>
> Now I appreciate him and acknowledge what he does that works. I can even acknowledge what he does that does not work and have a positive conversation about that. My husband is so much happier and so am I!

Just like with your children, acknowledgement tells your partner that you are here for them, that you believe in them, and that you are in their corner. Why would you want to communicate anything different to your partner?

REINFORCE THE POSITIVE

Acknowledgement is a great way to reinforce positive behaviors. When your partner does something you like, something you would like to see repeated, acknowledge them for it! Make them really feel your acknowledgement, put some "wow" into it. Then acknowledge them again the next time they do it! "You took out the trash!" "You remembered our anniversary!" "You vacuumed the house!" "You cleaned up after dinner!" "You picked up my dry cleaning!"

Remember, acknowledgement can be just as effective for little things. Do not wait for your partner to do something big. Acknowledge the little things ~ and the big things. Then you will get to watch your partner become happier and more inspired while your relationship gets stronger and stronger.

TWO-PERSON TEAM MEETINGS

Team meetings are also an excellent way to bring the practice of acknowledgement into your relationship. You can recognize what your partner did in the moment or the recent past.

After you and your partner have created a firm foundation of acknowledging each other, you may even be able to use acknowledgement to clean up the distant past by acknowledging something that was done in the past.

Normally, it would be awkward to out-of-the-blue recognize something your partner did years ago, especially if it was something you failed to acknowledge or recognize at the time it happened. Acknowledgement affords that opportunity. You can say "Sweetie, you got us caught up on our taxes five years ago." Or "You found this house for us" ~ and your partner will get it.

Remember, you need to have a strong foundation of acknowledgement before you dive into the distant past. But once you do have that strong foundation, you can acknowledge just about anything.

The team meeting creates an opportunity for you to clean up your history.

Often, when people acknowledge one another for the things they have been beating each other over the head with for years; they can finally let it go. The relationship can immediately become more about the present moment, rather than the past. That alone can heal many relationships.

I have seen many relationships end because people could not communicate with their partner effectively, without judgment and with appreciation. I believe that in some cases those relationships could have been saved if both parties had embraced the tool of acknowledgement before all trust was lost.

At the same time, good relationships can become even better with the tool of acknowledgement. As Sarah said, she believes that acknowledgement gives her and her husband the opportunity to be so much happier together.

RELATIONSHIP JUMP-START EXERCISE

Do you want to jump-start your relationship? Write down a list of ten things you would like to acknowledge your partner for. These could be current things or recent history.

Then have a two-person team meeting and acknowledge your partner. Remember; give one acknowledgement at a time. Let it land and be absorbed before you deliver the next acknowledgement.

If this seems like too big a step, that is okay. Do the first step ~ write down a list of things to acknowledge your partner for. Then just slowly start delivering those acknowledgements, one at a time in normal conversation.

For example, here is my list:

- ❖ Took out the trash
- ❖ Walked the dog
- ❖ Worked 60 hours this week
- ❖ Gave the kid a bath
- ❖ Cooked dinner last night
- ❖ Took the car to get the oil changed
- ❖ Reconciled the bank account
- ❖ Got a new client
- ❖ Took a day off and went skiing
- ❖ Vacuumed the house

I know what you are thinking. This is weird and impersonal to acknowledge these types of things. Almost everyone thinks that at first. Your partner may even ask, "What the heck are you up to?"

Don't let that deter you. Stick with it. This kind of acknowledgement will positively impact your relationship and much sooner than you think. Frequent acknowledgement will cause your relationship to become stronger than it is now.

WEIRD BUT EFFECTIVE

My client, Camden, a business consultant, decided to give acknowledgement a try in his relationship.

At first his wife thought the team meetings and acknowledgement in general were weird and forced. She kept waiting to hear "Thank You."

However, Camden stuck with it and kept giving acknowledgements and asking his wife what she wanted to be acknowledged for.

His wife still thinks that it is weird ~ and she likes the results it has created in their relationship.

She described her experience as very powerful and has noticed their connection has deepened and they have much more appreciation as well as tolerance for each other.

Camden said, "There is more togetherness in our family now ~ between me and my wife and also with our kids. We have just naturally started to spend more time together."

Camden was able to use acknowledgment to make a good relationship even better. It is important to note that even when his wife was initially resistant to using the tool, Camden did not let that deter him. He hung in there with her and stayed with it long enough for her to see and feel the results.

I see this happen the majority of the time when people implement acknowledgement. At first it is awkward. The awkwardness is soon overridden by the positive results acknowledgement produces.

WHY IS THIS GUY DIFFERENT?

A few years ago, I had a client whom I'll call Sue. Sue was a successful entrepreneur who had attended a few of my classes. In one of those classes, she learned acknowledgement and had successfully integrated it into her professional conversations.

A few months later, Sue began dating a new guy. She noticed that this guy was so much more receptive and interested in her than the other men she had dated.

I asked her what she was doing differently with him. She said, "Nothing, except I acknowledge him all the time."

I burst out laughing and said "Yes, and the more you acknowledge him, the more he will want to be with you." I continued to say, "I would be careful with all of that acknowledgement, unless you think you want to marry him."

I will let you in on a little secret. People choose who they spend time with based on how they feel about themselves when they are around that person. If they feel good about themselves when they are around you, they will want to spend as much time as they can with you.

RELATIONSHIP SECRET WEAPON

When you acknowledge people, they feel good about themselves and they associate that "feeling good about themselves" with being around you.

On a scale of 1 – 10, how would you rate your connection with your partner right now? And, what would you like it to be?

If there is a gap between these two numbers, acknowledgement is a great option to close this gap. When your partner consistently feels good about him or herself when around you, your connection will naturally increase.

How many relationship issues would increased connection solve? Would this build a stronger relationship and increase meaningful interaction? Would this create more intimacy?

The answer to all these questions is YES! I strongly believe acknowledgement can be your secret weapon, supporting you to create an enjoyable, fulfilling, and high-quality relationship.

Give acknowledgement a try in your relationship ~ like Camden, Sarah, and Sue did ~ and see what happens. Stick with it even if it is a little awkward at first.

CHAPTER FOURTEEN

Acknowledgement In Sales

Even if you think you are not a "salesperson" ~ you are. Everyone sells sometimes. Any time you have to influence people, get something done, or get what you want, sales is involved. There is an element of selling in many of our tasks and activities. So even if you resist the idea that you are in some way selling, I believe you can still glean something useful from this chapter.

Acknowledgement is a really powerful tool to use in the context of selling. One of the reasons it is so valuable in selling is because prospects are becoming more and more sensitive to the use of old-school, traditional sales techniques. Acknowledgement, on the other hand, gives you an option to create an authentic, respectful connection with your potential new client.

People are so tired of manipulative selling techniques that in the face of them, they automatically become resistant. Even if you do not intend to create resistance in your sales meetings, you probably are. As I have stated before, acknowledgement always creates receptivity. So, instead of the tired old strategy of overcoming a prospect's resistance, now you have a better strategy! Create some receptivity.

Acknowledgement warms your potential client up to you. In essence, it gets you on the same side of the table as

147

the client. When you acknowledge them, they feel good about themselves. Because they feel better about themselves when you are around, they automatically like you more, which makes it more likely they will do business with you.

Think about it for a minute. When you acknowledge someone, what is the message you send? The message is that someone is really paying attention to him or her. This creates a "Wow" experience.

When you pay enough attention to find something to acknowledge someone for, and then you actually acknowledge him or her, you get his or her attention. Plus, you look like a genius.

You stand out because most others are not paying deep, authentic attention to the people they are selling to. People's response to this type of attention is very positive.

When people feel acknowledged, they light up, and when people light up, they write checks. When people feel it is about you, they do not light up and they do not write checks.

Beware. This is an easy place to make acknowledgement more complicated than it really is. There are no special secret sales acknowledgements that you must learn.

Just listen to the other person! They will tell you what they have done and then you can acknowledge them.

Your prospect says, "I've spent two years looking at various solutions." You say, "You have looked for solutions for two years."

Your prospect says, "I am ready for a change." You say, "You have decided you are ready for a change."

Your prospect says, "I have been pulling my hair out; I do not know what to do." You say, "You have been pulling your hair out."

Your prospect says, "I've doubled my income in the last three years." You say, "You doubled your income."

This is not rocket science. Do not make it harder than it is.

Having said that, in order to make this work, you do have to be paying attention to what the prospect says. If you are busy trying to figure out what to say or do next, or what part of your script to recite, you will not hear the opportunities for acknowledgement.

PEOPLE BUY FROM PEOPLE THEY LIKE

The RAIN Group's publication, *How Clients Buy: 2009 Benchmark Report on Professional Services Marketing and Selling from the Client Perspective*, shows that the likeability element factors strongly in the decision-making process. Simply stated, people like to buy from people they like.

Twenty-five percent of the prospective buyers surveyed reported that they experienced having no personal chemistry with sellers. Eighty-six percent of these same buyers said they would be much more likely to consider purchasing from the seller if some kind of personal chemistry was established.

These survey results show the need to build real rapport and create chemistry cannot be overstated.

Acknowledgement is one of the most powerful ways to create chemistry and connection with another person quickly and, most importantly, with integrity.

It is important to note that for acknowledgement to really work well in sales, you need to come from a place of genuine acknowledgement and curiosity. Otherwise, you are just trying to use another form of manipulation, they will feel that, and they will not appreciate it. You need to be acknowledging them because you can, not to get somewhere.

If this somehow does not add up for you, it is probably because you have a distorted view of selling. We are talking about Professional Selling, which we define as: "Finding out what someone really wants and then assisting him or her to get it." This is very different than amateur selling. Amateur selling is what you think of when you think of distasteful or high-pressure selling. Amateur selling is the opposite of professional selling. It is fraught with tricks and manipulation. Amateur selling says, "Here is what I have, here is why you should buy it even though I do not know anything about you or your real wants, needs, and desires." It almost always creates resistance. Acknowledgement does not work in an environment of manipulation.

Remember, the best reason to acknowledge is because you can!

ACKNOWLEDGEMENT MAKES SELLING ENJOYABLE

Sarah, the Image and TV Expert, used to hate to sell. That was before she learned the tool of acknowledgement.

According to Sarah, "When I added acknowledgement to my sales conversation, I and my prospective clients started to have fun in the sales process. They became receptive and curious and interested. My closing rate skyrocketed. Now I look forward to and enjoy selling. Wow! Who knew that was possible!"

My client Doug, who owns a carpet cleaning service, had an experience similar to Sarah's experience when he started using acknowledgement in his sales.

Doug said, "I became so much more relaxed and comfortable in the sales process when I started using acknowledgement. I attribute this to the fact that I got my attention off of myself. Now instead of wondering how I am doing or being concerned about whether I am doing it right, I am really paying attention to the other person. I am looking to see who that person really is and what they want to be acknowledged for. This has made the conversations so much more enjoyable for me and also more effective."

Nancy, an award-winning entrepreneur, successful sales professional and founder of The Business Book Club, shares how she successfully uses acknowledgement in emails to help her sell. "Acknowledging people is one secret to my success. Every email presents a new opportunity to move a relationship forward. When you place yourself in another person's world and envision their environment, it's easy to focus on them and take yourself out of the picture. Once you grab their attention with a provocative subject line, leading the message with a personal acknowledgement of something he or she has done or said helps you make a connection. Subliminal or not, it's a genuine connection. When you keep the message short and simple with clear ideas about what you're committing to and what you are requesting, you can hit the send key with confidence that you are moving your relationship forward and a reply will soon be on its way."

CUSTOMER SERVICE

Even if you do not have a job in customer service, you will likely find yourself in a customer service role at some point. If you really think about it, most people in your life are your customer ~ in one way or another. Look and see how you can apply these ideas elsewhere in your life.

CUSTOMER SERVICE AND SALES

Some people think customer service is a completely different function than sales. Others see customer service as a part of sales.

Either way, customer service impacts your business and your profitability. The better you are at customer service, the more repeat sales you will make, the more referral sales you will receive, and the more potentially lost sales you will save.

Acknowledgment works just as well in customer service as it does in sales. Customer service can encompass many different types of interactions from helping customers with their purchases to dealing with complaints.

THREE TYPES OF CUSTOMER SERVICE

There are three main types of customer service situations: service based, assistance based, and complaint based.

In service based customer service, the customers are there to be served. This happens in restaurants, salons, spas, boutique retail establishments, air travel, and the like. The customer expects great, attentive service.

If waiters and waitresses found a way to acknowledge their customers, their tips would increase significantly. People make many decisions about where to buy, how to spend their time, how to spend their money, and in this case how much to tip, based on how they feel about themselves when they are with you. I know I do this when I am making a decision about how much to tip.

Airlines have a bigger problem; people are sometimes grumpy when they get on airplanes. I hope you have learned by now that just one or two simple acknowledgements can change that. You do not even have to be the flight attendant. If the person sitting next to you is grumpy, find something to acknowledge him or her for. It does not cost you anything and it might make the day better for both of you.

In assistance based customer service, the customer service associate is there to assist customers by providing information or help with purchases. Examples of this are electronic stores, home improvement stores, department stores, and the like.

153

Customers seek out help when they need some advice or expertise. Otherwise they tend to avoid interacting with the associates. Why is that?

While the customer expects quality assistance and guidance in these environments, the customer service is rarely stellar and often lack luster.

Part of the reason for this is the associate rarely takes the time to really connect with the customer and make them feel like more than just another guy looking for plumbing supplies, or another woman looking for an inexpensive pair of shoes.

Literally just one acknowledgment can make a customer feel heard, appreciated, and much more than just another number.

In complaint based customer service, the customer service associate is there to help people get their problem solved. Even if the customer service associate is able to help you with the problem, the experience is usually not enjoyable.

Again, if these associates were trained to give even one acknowledgement, the customer experience would be greatly improved.

COMPLAINTS

Upset or complaining customers and clients can happen anywhere at any time. Consequently, sales people and customer service associates have an opportunity to deal with complaints.

I say "opportunity" because these situations are an opportunity, not just to resolve the complaint, but to make the customer feel good about their decision to use your services or buy your product in the first place. If you turn the complaint around, the customer may even return to do business with you again.

Acknowledgment can be extremely helpful when people need assistance or are upset. Just a little bit of genuine acknowledgement can change the whole situation. The key is to really listen to the customer and find just a couple of simple things to acknowledge him or her for.

WHY THEY COMPLAIN

When people complain, they really only want one thing. They want to be heard. They are feeling unappreciated, unrecognized, under-valued, or under-served. They have an unresolved situation and want you to care about the situation and about them.

Most people respond to complaints in a way that does not make the person feel valued and appreciated, seen and heard. The person with the complaint does not get the message that the situation is as important to the customer service associate as it is to them. This is made even worse when the complaint receiver takes it personal or responds in a way that the customer feels patronized.

THE SOLUTION TO COMPLAINTS

In one word, the solution is ~ acknowledgement. Acknowledgement stops complaining and redirects the complaint to a productive track where a solution can be found and all parties end up having a positive experience.

STANDING OUT

Unfortunately, good customer service is the exception not the rule. So when we experience good customer service, it really stands out. Adding acknowledgement to your customer service strategy will cost you virtually nothing and it will immediately improve your customer's experience.

No matter what you call it or what your role, learning to acknowledge in any sales or customer service situation will pay huge dividends. Do yourself and all of your customers a big favor and give it a try.

There is so much more to be said about this topic that it could be its own book. As I have said, acknowledgement moves people. So for now, practice acknowledging in your sales process and customer service interactions and watch what happens.

CHAPTER FIFTEEN

Acknowledgement In Peak Performance

Acknowledgement is a key factor in assisting people to move into high or peak performance in any arena.

People already have what they need to succeed inside of them. Our job is simply to help them discover it so that they can see it, believe it, and take action around it. Richard Florida, author of *The Rise of The Creative Class*, said that people do not need to be managed. They need to be unleashed.

If that statement scares you, it should. Most of what you have been taught about human performance and motivation is dead wrong. If you have been taught that people need to be managed, then unleashing them is a radical new viewpoint.

If what we have been taught is wrong, what do we do? What is the answer?

TRADITIONAL MOTIVATION

Traditional forms of motivation do not work! Yet, over and over, people are trying to motivate other people.

Companies pay big bucks to motivational speakers to come in and motivate their workers.

The motivation provided by these speakers works, to a degree. People get fired up for a few days, and then they go back to business as usual. Why? Because motivation is an inside job. No matter how hard we try, we cannot create permanent motivation from the outside in.

If you have ever been to one of these events, you know what I am talking about. You are all enthusiastic for a few days and then it fades and you are left feeling sort of tired and hung over – and definitely not motivated.

And here is where it gets a little crazy. Because you believe the motivation myth, you think something is wrong with you. Something must be wrong with you because you were so fired up, but then it all disappeared.

Nothing is wrong with you! You just have a faulty belief that you should be motivated by someone or something else. This can only come from within you!

The problem with external motivation is that it is someone trying to motivate someone else! It is something being done to the person. It is an outside force acting on them, trying to provide a reason why they should act in a certain way. Most of the time, motivation is used in an attempt to get people to do something they do not want to do.

Also, motivation is really about the motivator, not the motivatee. This dynamic will almost always create resistance. Resistance and inspired action cannot coexist. Consequently, motivation seldom produces the desired results.

Managers, coaches, bosses, etc., usually think they are paid to motivate and make sure their people perform up to their capacity and capabilities. They think this is their job.

Parents, friends, and partners think it is their responsibility to motivate their kids, friends, or partners.

I strongly disagree. Their job is to be a lifeguard on the ocean of potential, rescuing people from the depths of fatigue and breathing life back into their dreams and desires. Said less poetically, I believe their job is to believe in people's potential, supporting them to unleash their brilliance and magnificence.

Unfortunately, this is not what usually happens. The results of current motivation practices are a far cry from assisting people to operate to their full potential.

WHY PEOPLE UNDERPERFORM

People underperform for one of two reasons: either they are not getting what they really want, or they are not getting enough acknowledgement. (Maybe those two are one and the same?) Either way, even adults will act out, pull attention, and cause drama when they do not feel acknowledged.

You know that drama queen or king at work? Yes, the one who drives you crazy. Why do you suppose they are that way? Usually, it is because they are not receiving enough acknowledgement.

At first, this might not make sense to you because they seem to be getting plenty of attention when they act up and are being dramatic. However, there is a difference between acknowledgement and attention. Acknowledgement provides attention but attention does not necessarily provide acknowledgement. People want to feel valued and appreciated and attention alone does not provide this.

Consequently, even though this person is receiving a lot of attention, they still keep acting up because their real need is not getting fulfilled. Negative attention does not make a person feel valued or appreciated. At the deepest level, people desire acknowledgement.

If someone, anyone, would start acknowledging him or her, and keep it up; the drama will substantially subside and maybe even stop. The challenge is most people say, "Why would I acknowledge them when all they do is go around trying to get attention?"

This statement is really just your judgment coming through. As I have said many times, judgment does not serve anyone. Just get in there, acknowledge them, and see what happens. Really, try it and see what happens.

What you are paying attention to directly influences what other people are paying attention to. You have a choice here: pay attention to their drama or pay attention to their performance and potential. When you choose performance and potential, you will be amazed by the results they can produce when someone believes in them.

PYGMALION EFFECT

Robert Rosenthal performed a well-known psychology experiment. His team gave intelligence tests to students in an elementary school. The teachers were then told which students had the greatest potential. The teachers were also instructed to not mention the study or to treat these students any different than the other students.

At the end of the school year, they tested the students again. As expected, the previously identified students exhibited great intellectual ability.

Here is where it gets interesting. The selected students were not identified because of how well they did on the first test. They were selected because of how average they were on the first test. The researchers lied to the teachers about the ability of these selected students.

Even though the teachers treated these students the same as the other students and never said anything about it, their belief in these students' potential got communicated anyway.

The teachers' belief transformed these ordinary students into academic wonder kids.

There is even a name for this phenomenon, The Pygmalion Effect. In *The Happiness Advantage*, Shawn Achor defines it as, "When our belief in another person's potential brings that potential to life."

Acknowledgement is the most direct, effective, and efficient way to pour our belief into another person.

In his book *Quiet Leadership*, David Rock says, "If we want to transform people's performance we need to master the skill of acknowledgement. This means building new mental wiring around seeing what people are doing well. It means watching . . ."

It is pretty straightforward really ~ to create better performance, we want people's attention on what is working. That way they can do more of the same. We want to reinforce positive behavior. That is exactly what acknowledgement does! This requires us to put our attention on them and really see them and what they are up to.

ESCAPE FROM MISERY AND UNDERPERFORMANCE

My client, Kathi Crawford, the founder and president of People Possibilities LLC, an innovative training and development firm, shares her experience of how acknowledgement moved her out of misery and underperformance.

> A few years ago I was really in a place of desperation and fear. I knew I needed to make a change in my career but I had a great job.
>
> In our culture it really isn't socially acceptable to leave a good job, no matter how miserable you are. I was stuck in that situation but I knew that I had to get off of the roller coaster I was on called 'Corporate America'. I was looking for a lifeline.
>
> At that time I noted in my journal: 'In my current situation I often go to work with a pit in my stomach. ... I am not happy or excited for the most part ...'
>
> I started working with Mattison not really knowing what to expect or how it would work. I was curious enough to give it a chance. At the same time I was defensive, resistant and a real pain in the ***.
>
> Mattison did not defend, she did not try to convince me of anything, or say 'have you tried this?' or 'In my opinion ...' In a

nutshell she never tried to overcome my resistance, which was very smart, because I was pretty dug in. I had my situation well defended and was ready to fight back.

At the same time I was not sure what she was doing but it didn't matter because I could not get enough. I felt good before, during and after every meeting. Almost immediately things began to change for me. I felt more confident, accepted, believed in, and downright powerful! The obstacles I had started vanishing one by one, replaced by ever increasing curiosity, receptivity, and excitement about what could happen. The defensiveness and resistance I harbored disappeared. I could now see that I had the ability to choose the direction I wanted to go. And ultimately I did.

Later I found out what Mattison actually did in our sessions. It was not magic, manipulation, or pressure. It was not appreciation, compliments, or praise.

It was acknowledgement, acknowledgement, and more acknowledgement. And that created tremendous positive change in my life and in my career.

Acknowledgement will absolutely help you get results. It will help you to both support and unleash others to perform at high levels. However, it is important to remember that you cannot bring a right or wrong, good or bad, context to it. Acknowledgement by definition is without judgment, whether that is a judgment of good or a judgment of bad.

Tony Schwartz is the president and CEO of The Energy Project. He says, "At the emotional level, our core need is to feel safe, secure and valued . . . The more attentive we are to meeting these core needs, the less likely we are to feel overwhelmed and exhausted, and the more sustainably high-performing we're capable of becoming." Acknowledgement makes people feel safe, secure, and valued.

THE CURSE OF THE
HIGH PERFORMER

The curse of the high performer is that high performers often do not acknowledge or even recognize what they have done well. They do not see, much less celebrate, their successes. They get something done and then "step over it." They do not acknowledge or collect their just rewards for a job well done. They think and tell themselves, "It is no big deal."

On the other hand, they spend a lot of time worrying about what did not work. This is not a recipe for happiness nor does it produce balance. If we do not acknowledge our successes, pretty soon we begin to feel like we are not having any. We end up like Val (Chapter 11), focused on all the things that are not working, instead of the things that are.

This phenomenon is often present in high performers and hinders their ability to perform at even higher levels. It also negatively impacts the quality of their lives.

Fortunately, there is a cure for this curse and I bet you can guess what it is.

Acknowledgement is the cure for the curse of the high performer.

Vic Zachary, former Army Ranger and owner of Bayou City CrossFit, describes how he saw the curse of the high performer show up in some of his teammates during training and competition.

> We had two women on the team that could not see the positive in themselves. They always saw the negative and you could see that attitude in their workouts. After the training sessions, when their teammates would say 'Hey, great job', they would argue with the praise. They would say things like, 'No, I was slow' or 'I didn't lift as much weight as I wanted to.'
>
> Once we started having team meetings and acknowledging them, things changed. We were able to point out things that they had not even noticed in themselves or else had discounted. After the acknowledgements, their demeanor and even their body language changed. Small, hunched-over shoulders changed to standing tall with their chests open and their heads held higher.

I cannot stress enough the value of acknowledgement in helping people find and maintain peak performance. The best part is that it is really simple, does not take a long time, and can easily be implemented into almost any situation.

I return to the bold statement I made in Chapter 2 ~ Acknowledgement has the power to produce magical results. It is up to you to get out there and use it. When you do, people's lives will change.

I use this tool of acknowledgement so much in my coaching practice. Over and over again, I have seen it unleash people! They go from being stuck into taking massive action towards their dreams and desires. Acknowledgement moves people and teams into the realm of peak performance like nothing else I know of.

CHAPTER SIXTEEN

Because You Can

I cannot count how many times I have seen people struggle with the frustration of underperformance, lack of attention and appreciation, and just flat out confusion.

Managers and functional leaders struggle with how to get the best out of their people. They often attempt to do this by improving technologies. If we just had better software, or better equipment, or a better mousetrap, then our people could do better. Yet, with all the technological advances we have, people are not fundamentally performing better.

This is because you cannot solve a human problem with a technological solution. You have to solve human problems with a human solution. And unlike software programs, Standard Operating Procedures, performance improvements processes, or Six Sigma, acknowledgement is not a program or an activity. Acknowledgement is a tool, a tool used by human beings to improve other human beings.

The best thing about acknowledgement is that it can be used in just about any situation, without having to make massive, sweeping changes to most of what you already have in place. It fits in anywhere, as a human solution to a most human problem.

167

When I first started using acknowledgement, it changed my relationship to my mouth ~ well, at least to the words coming out of my mouth.

This happened because I really grasped the distinction of acknowledgement. This now allows me to be much clearer about what I am trying to accomplish when I speak. Is my intention to give attention to the other person and be a wind in their sail, or is my intention to put my attention on myself and on what I like, appreciate, and find valuable? Is the conversation about them or about me? The answer to that question allows me to choose the appropriate communication tool.

Since my interest is in contributing to others and assisting them to fulfill their dreams and desires, I acknowledge.

I still do that other stuff ~ liking, appreciating, finding valuable ~ in my own head. What comes out of my mouth is acknowledgement.

ACKNOWLEDGEMENT MOVES PEOPLE

Acknowledgement moves people, motivates them, and opens the door to high levels of performance. I have built a successful career around acknowledgement. I feel like if I just notice and acknowledge, clarify and make distinctions, and then acknowledge some more, I can create massive value for people. In my experience, people are very willing to pay for this value (opening the door to high-level performance) that I can create through acknowledgement.

Furthermore, it is a pleasure to do the acknowledging and it is a pleasure to get acknowledged. This puts the whole interaction on the pleasure channel. This stands out because it is not "business as usual." Far too many interactions in a person's daily life are not pleasurable or enjoyable.

If you consistently implement acknowledgement in your life, business, relationships, and career, you will consistently improve your results and the results of the people around you.

If somebody came to me and said, "We are taking away every tool in your communication toolbox except one. Which one do you want to keep?" Guess which one I would keep? I can contribute more to another person with acknowledgement than I can with all my other tools . . . combined!

In order for acknowledgement to become a natural part of your communication, you need to do a lot of it. Go out and do a lot of it! Your friends, family, and co-workers will love you for it.

MY CHALLENGE TO YOU

Remember, if you choose to accept this assignment, your mission is to deliver ten acknowledgements a day for the rest of your life!

FINAL THOUGHT

The best reason ~ and ultimately the real reason ~ to acknowledge people is simply because you can. You have a tool in your possession that can change lives. You can assist people to improve their performance, increase their self-confidence, and positively impact the people around them. Through acknowledgement you can support people to live happier and more fulfilling lives.

Now that you have this powerful tool, it is my hope that you will use it whenever and wherever possible. Over time, acknowledgement will become one of your most valuable people skills. That transition may take some time and effort; however, the return on your investment is well worth it. In all my years of using acknowledgement, I have never seen sincere acknowledgement fail to increase the capacity of another human being.

You now have the power and the ability to increase the capacity of others and contribute to them on a profound level whenever you choose. I sincerely hope that you choose to do this often!

Works Cited

THE MYTH

Gostick, Adrian Robert, and Chester Elton. 2007. *The carrot principle: How the best managers use recognition to engage their people, retain talent, and accelerate performance.* New York: Free Press.

Rath, Tom, and Donald O. Clifton. 2004. *How full is your bucket?: Positive strategies for work and life.* New York: Gallup Press.

Society for Human Resource Management (U.S.), and SHRM Foundation. 2000. *Retention practices survey.* Alexandria, Va.: Society for Human Resource Management: SHRM Foundation.
Stevenson, Robert. 2010. *The power of appreciation.* Customer management blog. http://www.icmi.com/Blog/2010/ November/The-Power-of-Appreciation ed.International Customer Management Institute (accessed 11/2011).

COMPLIMENTS, PRAISE, AND APPRECIATION DO NOT WORK

Achor, Shawn. 2010. *The happiness advantage: The seven principles of positive psychology that fuel success and performance at work.* New York: Broadway Books.

Anthony, Robert. 2006. *The ultimate secrets of total self-confidence.* New York: Berkley Books.

Bronson, Po. February 11, 2007. *How not to talk to your kids, the inverse power of praise*. New York Magazine, http://nymag.com/news/features/27840/ (accessed 11/2011). Bronson, Po, and Ashley Merryman. 2009. *NurtureShock*. NurtureShock: New thinking about children. New York: Twelve.

Dweck, C. S. 2002. Messages that motivate: How praise molds students' beliefs, motivation, and performance (in surprising ways). In *Improving academic achievement: Impact of psychological factors on education (educational psychology).*, ed. Joshua Michael Aronson. Amsterdam; Boston: Academic Press.

Levy, Shawn. 2009. *Paul Newman: A life*. New York: Harmony Books.

Maltz, Maxwell, and Larry Wilson. 1990. *Psychocybernetics*. Queensland: Seminar Company.

Rock, David,. 2006. *Quiet leadership: Help people think better -- don't tell them what to do: Six steps to transforming performance at work*. New York: Collins.

ACKNOWLEDGEMENT ~ WHAT IT IS AND WHAT IT IS NOT

Achor, Shawn. 2011. *TEDxBloomington -"The happiness advantage: Linking positive brains to performance"*. The wisdom of play., eds. Kaylynn Huffman Brower, Rob Anderson. http://www.youtube.com/watch?v=GXy__kBVq1M; ed. Vol. 2011. Bloomington, Indiana: IU Radio and Television Services (accessed 2011).

Rock, David,. 2006. *Quiet leadership: Help people think better -- don't tell them what to do: Six steps to transforming performance at work*. New York: Collins.

HOW TO ACKNOWLEDGE

Nyad, Diana. Diana Nyad: Extreme dream: Off camera at the today show. 2011. Available from http://diananyad.com/off-camera-at-the-today-show/ (accessed 11/2011).

SELF-ACKNOWLEDGEMENT

Achor, Shawn. 2010. *The happiness advantage: The seven principles of positive psychology that fuel success and performance at work.* New York: Broadway Books.

Sandler, David H. 1995. *You can't teach a kid to ride a bike at a seminar.* New York: Dutton.

ACKNOWLEDGEMENT IN LEADERSHIP

Amabile, Teresa M., and Steven J. Kramer. January - February, 2010. *The HBR list: Breakthrough ideas for 2010.* Harvard business review: The magazine. http://hbr.org/2010/01/the-hbr-list-breakthrough-ideas-for-2010/ar/1 ed. Cambridge, Massachusetts: Harvard Business School Publishing Corporation (accessed 11/2011).

Pink, Daniel H. 2009. *Drive: The surprising truth about what motivates us.* New York, NY: Riverhead Books.

Rath, Tom, and Donald O. Clifton. 2004. *How full is your bucket?: Positive strategies for work and life.* New York: Gallup Press.

Schwartz, Tony. 2011. *There's no such thing as constructive criticism.* HBR blog network. http://blogs.hbr.org/schwartz/2011/11/theres-no-such-thing-as-constr.html ed. Cambridge,

Massachusetts: Harvard Business Publishing (accessed 11/2011).

ACKNOWLEDGEMENT IN SALES

RAIN Group. 2009. *How clients buy: 2009 benchmark report on professional services marketing and selling from the client perspective*RainToday.com and Wellesley Hills Group, LLC.

ACKNOWLEDGEMENT IN PEAK PERFORMANCE

Achor, Shawn. 2010. *The happiness advantage: The seven principles of positive psychology that fuel success and performance at work.* New York: Broadway Books.

Florida, Richard L. 2002. *The rise of the creative class: And how it's transforming work, leisure, community and everyday life.* New York, NY: Basic Books.

Rock, David,. 2006. *Quiet leadership: Help people think better -- don't tell them what to do: Six steps to transforming performance at work.* New York: Collins.

Rosenthal, Robert, and Lenore Jacobson. 1968. *Pygmalion in the classroom.* Irvington, New York: Holt, Rinehart & Winston.

Schwartz, Tony. 2011. *Is the life you're living worth the price you're paying to live it?.* HR blog network. http://blogs. hbr.org/schwartz/2011/07/is-the-life-youre-living-worth.html ed. Cambridge, Massachusetts: Harvard Business School Publishing (accessed 11/2011).

About The Authors

MATTISON GREY

Mattison Grey, M.Ed. is a Leadership and Performance Specialist and the world's foremost authority on acknowledgement and communication. Since 1997, Mattison has been coaching teams and individuals and consulting in organizations in the areas of leadership, communication, sales, team work, and high performance.

Mattison is a professional member of the National Speakers Association and speaks frequently about leadership, performance, and developing the skills necessary to bring out the best in others. Her clients and audiences enjoy her innovative views on human performance and her courage to be provocative in ways that challenges the status quo.

As a professionally-certified business coach, Mattison has helped thousands of people create extraordinary lives and businesses. She is fascinated by the gap between high performers and low performers and what it takes to go from mediocre to masterful in a chosen endeavor.

Mattison lives in Houston, Texas with her family and two dogs. She is an avid Touch Rugby Player and Crossfitter.

For more information about speaking engagements, training, and consulting go to: www.mattisongrey.com.

JONATHAN MANSKE

Jonathan Manske is the world's only Cerebral Sanitation Engineer. Since 1993, he has been working with individuals and organizations to upgrade the quality of their lives, relationships, health, businesses, and careers.

Jonathan has created his own body of work that first assists people to get clear about what they really want. Then he works with them to remove all of the self-imposed obstacles that are in their way ~ obstacles like: fear, limiting beliefs and perspectives, lack of confidence, lack of self-belief, poor self-image and other head trash.

His passion is to work with people to create happiness, fulfillment, prosperity, and wealth.

Jonathan is a professional speaker and trainer. He speaks frequently about the consciousness and psychology of success, how to get out of your own way so that you can unleash your inner top performer, and how to create happiness and upgrade quality of life. He loves to provide people with tools that they can easily use to produce positive and meaningful change in their lives.

Jonathan is also the author of *The Law of Attraction Made Simple* and *A Great Life Does Not Happen By Accident*.

He lives with his wife and daughter in Denver, Colorado. He is an avid volleyball player, mountainbiker, and fisherman.

For more information about Jonathan and about speaking engagements, training, and consulting go to: www.jonathanmanske.com.

Made in the USA
Las Vegas, NV
19 September 2021

30406610R00111